# D-Day Assault

*To Bea my partner and Aimee my daughter.*
*Thank you both for being there.*

# D-Day Assault

## The Second World War Assault Training Exercises at Slapton Sands

### Mark Khan

Pen & Sword
**MILITARY**

First published in Great Britain in 2014 by
Pen & Sword Military
an imprint of
Pen & Sword Books Ltd
47 Church Street
Barnsley
South Yorkshire
S70 2AS

Copyright © Mark Khan 2014

ISBN 978 1 78159 384 4

The right of Mark Khan to be identified as the Author of this Work has
been asserted by him in accordance with the Copyright, Designs and
Patents Act 1988.

A CIP catalogue record for this book is available from the British
Library

Typeset in Ehrhardt by
Mac Style Ltd, Bridlington, East Yorkshire
Printed and bound in the UK by CPI Group (UK) Ltd, Croydon,
CRO 4YY

Pen & Sword Books Ltd incorporates the imprints of Pen & Sword
Archaeology, Atlas, Aviation, Battleground, Discovery, Family
History, History, Maritime, Military, Naval, Politics, Railways, Select,
Transport, True Crime, and Fiction, Frontline Books, Leo Cooper,
Praetorian Press, Seaforth Publishing and Wharncliffe.

For a complete list of Pen & Sword titles please contact
PEN & SWORD BOOKS LIMITED
47 Church Street, Barnsley, South Yorkshire, S70 2AS, England
E-mail: enquiries@pen-and-sword.co.uk
Website: www.pen-and-sword.co.uk

# Contents

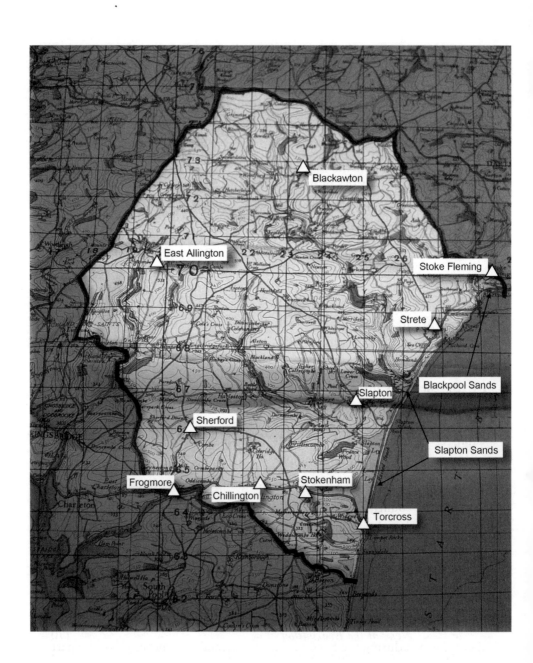

# Introduction

As a very small boy I used to be taken to Slapton Sands and on one occasion I remember playing on the beach and glanced down to find something lying on top of the shingle. The 'something' I had found was a spent .30 calibre cartridge case. Pleased with my find and curious as to what it was, I took it home. It was my introduction to collecting and to military history, particularly the military history of Slapton Sands. As a schoolboy in the 1970s living in the village of Blackawton, at the weekend I used to walk to the beach at Slapton Sands, a distance of roughly five miles each way. I would scour the beach area for more spent cartridge cases and built up a collection of these and other Second World War related items as well. Often I would be joined by a good friend from school and my big brother.

Over the years my curiosity grew and I began to look for information about how the various items I had found came to be there. Information at the time was hard to come by, even though the Second World War had occurred only thirty years previously.

Local people were often not keen to talk about a period of time that many of them would rather forget. Additionally, the peaceful South Hams, like much of the country in the late 1930s and early 1940s was a very different world than it is today. People were less worldly-wise and lived in many ways a simpler lifestyle. For many the changes that occurred during the war years seemed to be almost too much for them to cope with. Subsequently this seemed to lead to an unwillingness to speak about them.

In time I grew up and left the area, although I returned many times to visit, and eventually to live there again. Meanwhile I read and researched about the area during the Second World War, and became aware of the part it had played and of the many American soldiers who had been based in South Devon and trained at Slapton Sands.

A desire grew to 'do something' with the knowledge that I was acquiring. After many years, the opportunity finally came to do this. Working as a full-time military historian, the idea for this book was formed, to fill the gap in the recording of the true events that took place at Slapton Sands and their significance in relation to the outcome of the Second World War.

My original intention had been to focus on purely the military exercises. Much had already been written about the civilian evacuation of the South Hams, so I had not planned to cover this in any detail. However, once I started properly to research the subject, I became aware that the evacuation was an integral part of the story and needed to be included. It dawned on me how much fortitude had been shown by the evacuees and the important part that they played in unlocking the door of Hitler's fortress Europe. Further research uncovered stories of Government disdain and Treasury penny pinching towards those who had so willingly and uncomplainingly given up their homes and in many case suffered significant personal and financial loss. There were also those decent and fair-minded individuals who made the straightforward case that the people who had been evacuated must be treated fairly and properly looked after, and the story of how the Americans came to the rescue also came to light.

Slapton Sands is often mentioned in relation to the exercises that took place during January and May 1944. Unfortunately, this often focuses on the events of the night of 28 April 1944 when two landing craft where sunk and one badly damaged in Lyme Bay whilst en-route to take part in Exercise Tiger, resulting in a tragic loss of life. The story of the loss of the landing craft has become synonymous with Slapton Sands, and in the process the real story of the evacuation and the exercises and training that took place in the South Hams has become lost. The contribution that both the people and the area made to the success of the Normandy landings is often unrecognised, overshadowed by conspiracy theory, conjecture, plain misunderstanding or sometimes a deliberate misrepresentation of the facts. This book is an attempt to redress this and to tell the story of the area and its people and also to fully recognise the contribution they made to the success of D-Day and the subsequent victory against Nazi Germany.

The story of D-Day is well known and is not detailed in this book, having been covered in great detail elsewhere. To the men taking part, it had been a long journey. Mostly citizen soldiers, they fought together alongside their friends and comrades, providing mutual support to each other. Many were injured and many killed in the battles to liberate Nazi occupied Europe. Some of the story of D-Day may be better understood once this book is read; how it was shaped by the events that took place during the training, experimenting and the many assault landing exercises that took place at Slapton Sands and its hinterland. D-Day itself was an enormous task. It was not only a brilliant triumph on the day and the days that followed it, but also in its planning and preparation beforehand. The assault training was a major component of this.

Visiting the South Hams area today it is difficult to imagine the events that took place in 1944. It is a beautiful area with much to see and do. Its people are friendly, courteous and helpful. If reading this book informs, educates and entertains I will have done my job as an author. I would aspire to go one step further by encouraging people to visit the area and enjoy meeting the local people. The countryside is wonderful and there are many attractions to visit. If whilst visiting and after reading this book they also take a moment to think about the events of 1944 in their true context, free from controversy and conspiracy then I have truly succeeded in what I set out to do.

# Acknowledgements

No author is capable of producing a book without significant help from others. This has been said many times; it is now my turn to do so!

My first thanks must go to my wonderful partner Bea, who has supported me so well, putting up with the view of my back for hours on end while I have been connected by a seemingly invisible umbilical cord to my computer. Thanks also for taking my monosyllabic responses so well without appearing to get offended.

My good friend and colleague Martin Mace, has also been a fantastic source of support, advice and inspiration. Without it, this book would not have happened. John Grehan has also provided sterling service by acting as a sounding post and helping provide good advice. I must also thank Matt Jones at Pen and Sword for his patience in having to deal with me, and performing politely and professionally at all times. Thanks also to my editor, Barnaby Blacker, grandson of one of my all time heroes Lieutenant-Colonel Latham Valentine Stewart Blacker OBE.

My last thanks must go to my mother Ursula Khan. Not only was she responsible for ensuring that I arrived on this planet, but if it had not been for her decision to move the two of us to South Devon in 1968, I would never have had the reason to write this book. A writer herself, she died just before this book was completed.

*Chapter One*

# A History of Amphibious Operations

Examples of Military operations involving landing from the sea can be traced back to ancient times.

In 490 BC the Persians invaded Greece. Successfully landing by sea, the numerically superior Persians were defeated at the battle of Marathon – a bad result for the invading Persians.

Many years later, the Norman invasion of England would ultimately result in victory for the invading army of Duke William II of Normandy over the English army led by King Harold II – a better result this time for the invaders.

In the twentieth century, first amphibious operations occurred during the Russo–Japanese war in 1904 when a Japanese landing took place at Inchon in Korea, where forty-six years later another more famous amphibious landing would take place during the Korean War.

The First World War would feature the first major amphibious operation of the twentieth century at Gallipoli. By the time of the First World War the technology of warfare had reached an advanced state. The days when an invader simply had to run off a boat on to the shore had long gone. Modern artillery enabled targets to be accurately engaged, bolt-action rifles enabled high volumes of accurate rifle fire to be directed on the enemy, and the development of the machine gun could make life very difficult for an attacker. Advances in gunnery technology had made coastal guns a formidable opponent. Often looked on as a bit of a white elephant, coastal gunnery was a highly technical trade, many elements of which were eventually taken up by the gunners on land. The great Gunner and writer on artillery matters, Ian V. Hogg, visited the Coast Artillery School at the Citadel in Plymouth during the early 1950s as part of the Long Gunnery Staff Course he was attending. On the first day during the opening address, the instructor observed that the going rate in ammunition fired, for anti-aircraft artillery to hit a target, was approximately 1000 rounds per aircraft, field artillery invariably fired a few ranging rounds before getting on target; but coastal artillery hit the target with the first shot fired. Disinclined to believe this, Hogg describes how 'the next day we were taken to Renney Battery and watched a 6-inch gun blow a fast moving target out of the water with the first shot[1]'.

Today, the recognised requirements for a modern amphibious operation are:

- Sound, unambiguous political and strategic direction.
- Well-practiced joint staff procedures and careful selection of officers for key appointments.
- Well-trained and equipped land forces.
- Adequate weaponry and munitions.
- Thorough attention to logistics.
- Reliable intelligence based on the availability of good maps and charts and on thorough reconnaissance.
- Accurate assessment of enemy capabilities based on the foregoing intelligence.
- Appreciation of geographical and hydrographical factors affecting the projection of power over what may be extended distances[2].

At a higher level, the basis for military strategy is based on two concepts: manoeuvre and attrition. Manoeuvre is based on the ability to shatter your enemy's overall cohesion and will to fight by striking with shock and surprise and disrupting his will and ability to fight by hitting at the weakest point when he least expects it. Attrition is based on the idea of the reduction of an enemy force by causing loss of personnel and equipment.

Amphibious operations fit the manoeuvrist approach to warfare. They can also be broken down into two types of operation:

- Invasion – the intent to seize, hold, exploit, then advance into enemy territory.
- Raid – a short-term operation with a distinct aim resulting in a planned withdrawal.

Amphibious operations during World War Two can be split into two distinct theatres of operation, The European, Middle East and African theatre; and the Central Pacific Theatre. The operations carried out in these theatres varied dramatically and adopted distinct styles. Broadly speaking many were frontal assaults on heavily defended enemy territory. Some however were carried out deliberately avoiding frontal assaults. The specific manner in which all were carried out varied considerably and were dependent on the many factors affecting each one separately. There was no 'one size fits all' solution. In some cases, the desire for shock and surprise was defined by the manoeuvrist approach, was initially met during the initial landings, but turned into a campaign of attrition. To understand the context of Operation Overlord – the Normandy Landings – it helps to understand the history of amphibious operations up to that time. To that end I have detailed a brief history of amphibious warfare in the twentieth century up to May 1944. The concept of an amphibious invasion, whilst incredibly complex to plan and achieve basically comes down to two easily expressed problems:

To get ashore, and to stay ashore.

## Amphibious Operations in the First World War

The major amphibious operation commonly identified with the First World War is the campaign at Gallipoli. Launched due to the need for indirect action against the Central Powers and the Ottoman Empire and to aid a struggling Russia, the operations at Gallipoli have become synonymous with failure. The reasons cited for the failure of this operation were: a lack of a main aim or end point, appalling unsanitary conditions ashore, lack of security compromising the operation from the start, lack of concentration of force, poor inter-service integration, logistic unsustainability, lack of training, poor intelligence, and lack of control of the sea[3].

Recognising that this operation was not going to succeed, a highly successful withdrawal was achieved

On the night of 8–9 January 1916, 17,000 British soldiers were evacuated. In just over a week 35,000 soldiers, 3,689 horses and mules, 127 guns, 328 vehicles, and 1,600 tons of stores had been taken off. The failure of this campaign led to serious repercussions for its major proponents and for those in command.

Another lesser-known operation, Operation Albion, the invasion of the Ösel and Moon Islands, was carried out by the Germans in September 1917. Located in the northeast Baltic in what is now Estonia, these islands lie at the mouth of the Gulf of Riga. Fortified by the Russians, they prevented German naval forces attacking the strong Russian naval forces that operated from the Gulf. This amphibious operation was part of the German strategic offensive during 1917 to knock out a faltering Russia. A clear directive issued: 'To secure control of the Gulf of Riga and to guard the flank of the Ostheer, the islands of Ösel and Moon are to be taken through a coordinated attack by land and sea forces and the passage of enemy naval forces through Moon sound is to be blocked[4]'. On 12 October 1917 after a preliminary bombardment, the German assault force landed at Tagga Bay on the northwest of Ösel, and simultaneously near Pamerort a little further to the east.

The operation was a complete success. The Islands were captured in what was described by Brigadier General James Edward Edmonds CB CMG, responsible for the post-war compilation of the twenty-eight volume History of the Great War, as 'a model enterprise of its kind[5]'. Despite never having carried out an amphibious operation before, the Germans managed successfully to land a large force ashore in the face of opposition and quickly achieve their objectives. This operation proved that a successful amphibious operation could be carried out.

Another amphibious operation, Operation Zo, better known as the Zeebrugge Raid (and a raid rather than a longer-term landing), took place in April 1918. Early in 1917 the Germans had launched unrestricted submarine warfare, which produced extremely successful results with 800,000 tons of shipping being sunk by just 75 U-boats in April 1917. The convoy system was introduced in April 1917 to counter the U-boat threat. The Germans switched their U-boat attacks from deeper waters to shorter sea passages to Ireland or inshore coastal passages, particularly the English Channel where shipping was vulnerable whether sailing in or out of convoy. The majority of U-boats making attacks in British waters sailed from the port of Bruges, which was eight miles inland and connected to the coast by a series of canals, eventually emerging into the sea at Zeebrugge. Operation Zo was planned to block the Bruges canal and also to cause as much damage as possible to the port facilities at Ostend. The old cruiser HMS *Vindictive,* in company with other ships, was used as an assault vessel, and block ships were planned to be sunk to block the canal entrance. The attack took place late on 22 April. The attack was a failure as the block ships were not positioned to fully block the canal. The British experience of amphibious assault however, was added to.

In the years after the First World War, the main focus of the development of amphibious warfare switched to the Pacific. Increasing expansionist imperialism drove the development of amphibious warfare in Japan, engendering a counter-focus by the Americans, with their long Pacific west coast and other interests in the Philippines and Pacific bases.

With the outbreak of the Second World War, the first major amphibious operation was the German invasion of Norway. Operation Weserübung took place in the early hours of 9 April 1940. Taken by surprise, the British and Norwegians failed to successfully counter the attack. Despite the despatch of a joint British, Polish and French force to Norway, the campaign ended in success for the German invaders. The success of the German operations can be attributed to: unified planning and command, command of the air, having the necessary specialist troops and equipment to carry out the operation, the speed of decisions made during the operations, and the speed of the execution of the operation. It has been recognised that there was a significant risk to carrying out the operation, but good intelligence and a good logistic plan had helped mitigate these risks.

The next planned major amphibious operation was another German enterprise. Operation Sea Lion – the invasion of Mainland British Isles. This of course never took place. The failure of the Luftwaffe to obtain command of the air, the might of the British Navy, and the destruction of German amphibious capability by Bomber Command during the 'Battle of The Barges',[6] ensured that this operation was defeated before it even started.

During 1941 and 1942 a number of raiding operations were carried out, notably to the Lofoten Islands (Operation Claymore), Spitsbergen (Operations Gauntlet & Anklet) and Vaagso (Operation Archery). Amphibious operations were now under the banner of Combined Operations. Initially they were commanded by Admiral of the Fleet Sir

Roger Keyes from 17 July 1940 to 27 October 1941, and then by Lord Louis Mountbatten until August 1943. These raids, in contrast to many previous operations, were notable successes and demonstrated a growing ability to perform successful amphibious operations.

The first major Combined Operations amphibious landing, Operation Ironclad, the invasion of Madagascar, took place on 5 May 1942. Lying off the southeast coast of Africa in the Indian Ocean, the 1,000 mile long island was a French Colonial possession and in 1941 under the control of the Vichy government. Grave concern existed relating to Japanese intentions in the Indian Ocean. Should this island fall into Japanese hands it would pose a grave threat to Britain's communications to the Middle East. A pre-emptive occupation was therefore planned. The operation, carried out 9,000 miles away from Britain, was a success despite being carried out with limited resources. During this operation the British learned lessons and much experience was gained.

A major raid on the French port of St Nazaire, Operation Chariot, was carried out on 27 March 1942. Its aim was to destroy the Normandy dry dock, the only facility on the Atlantic coast that could offer repair facilities to German battleships. The old destroyer HMS *Campbeltown* was packed full of explosives and rammed against the dock gates. The delayed action charge exploded on 28 March destroying the dock gates which were never repaired for the rest of the war. A daring operation, the men involved fought with great courage and determination. Five Victoria Crosses were awarded for actions during this operation.

The next major amphibious operation was a controversial action. The Dieppe Raid, Operation Jubilee, was carried out on 18 August 1942. A raid in force, comprising 6,000 troops, attacked the French coastal town as a demonstration of offensive action and to appease Stalin's demands for the opening of a second front in Europe. The raid was a failure. Many of the troops were killed or captured, with particular losses being suffered by the courageous Canadian troops taking part. Chief of Combined Operations, Vice-Admiral Louis Mountbatten, the major advocate of this raid asserted that major lessons would be learned as a result of it.

The next major amphibious operation that took place was Operation Torch, the Anglo-American invasion of French North Africa, in November

1942. This was a large-scale operation involving three task forces. The Western Task Force sailed 3,900 miles from Norfolk, Virginia to assault the area around Casablanca; the Centre Task Force assaulted the area around Oran; and the Eastern Task Force assaulted Algiers. The assaulting forces, comprising approximately 125,000 men, successfully landed and proceeded to move westwards against the German Forces in North Africa. The largest and most ambitious amphibious operation so far in the war, this was a hugely complex operation aided specifically by the element of surprise backed up by a clever deception plan.

The drive to assault mainland Europe started on 10 July 1943 with Operation Husky, the invasion of Sicily. This operation involved 181,000 men, 14,000 vehicles, 600 tanks and 1,800 guns supported by a fleet of 3,200 ships landing on the southwestern and southeastern tip of the island[7]. After bitter fighting, the island was taken on 17 August, with the Germans withdrawing across the Straits of Messina to mainland Italy.

Following the successful invasion of Sicily the first operation to take mainland Europe took place on 9 September 1943 with Operation Avalanche and the landings at Salerno on the southern coast of Italy near Naples. In this operation 55,000 troops took part in the assault with a further 115,000 landing as part of the follow up operation[8]. Whilst the landing and securing of the beachhead was a success, the operation to breakout took longer than planned. General Bernard Montgomery stated 'In my view operation Avalanche was a good operation to carry out, but not enough effort had been put in to make it work'.[9]

The last amphibious assault prior to the Normandy landings in the European theatre, Operation Shingle, took place at Anzio on 22 January 1944. During the winter of 1943/44 the Allied advance had ground to a halt, held up by the German defences of the Gustav Line which ran from just north of where the Garigliano River flows into the Tyrrhenian Sea in the west, through the Apennine Mountains to the mouth of the Sangro River on the Adriatic coast in the east.

By landing behind the enemy lines it was hoped that the German commander in Italy, Field Marshal Albert Kesselring, would be forced to divide his forces to meet the multiple threats of the Anzio beachhead and the forces assaulting the Gustav Line.

The landing here failed to deliver the dynamic and decisive blow that it had hoped it would. Winston Churchill using his ability to eloquently describe situations, is reported to have commented 'I had hoped we were hurling a wildcat into the shore, but all we got was a stranded whale.'[10]

## Operations in the Pacific (1940–1944)

Shifting focus to the Pacific, a number of major amphibious operations were carried out by the Americans against the Japanese. Having declared war on Japan on 8 December 1942 as a result of the attack on Pearl Harbor on 7 December 1942, the Americans had been on the back foot against Japanese assaults on land, at sea and in the air. In August 1942 the Americans struck back at Guadalcanal in the Solomon Islands. Operation Watchtower was the first offensive amphibious operation carried out by American troops in the Second World War.

The operation was planned to stem the Japanese expansion and to prevent them building airfields on the Solomon Islands which would threaten shipping routes between the USA and Australia. A relentless battle was fought comprising a number of amphibious operations. As a result of the Americans isolating the Japanese from supply and re-enforcement, and a grinding war of attrition, organised resistance finally ended on 9 February 1943.

In May 1943, the Americans started the process of re-taking the Aleutian Islands from the Japanese by performing an amphibious assault on the Island of Attu in the Western Aleutians. Codenamed Operation Landcrab the assault started on 8 May 1943. Over 14,000 American troops took part in this operation. After the failure of a final assault by the Japanese, at Engineer Hill, resistance ended on 29 May. Mainly fought off by American support units, the 500 surviving Japanese committed suicide. Of the approximately 2,400 defending Japanese troops only 29 were captured alive.[11]

In November 1943, Operation Galvanic took place to wrest control of the Gilbert Islands from the Japanese. Located 4,900 km northeast of Australia, the Gilbert Islands comprise sixteen low-lying islands and atolls, none higher than four metres in elevation. Two simultaneous assaults took place at Tarawa Atoll and Makin Atoll on 20 November 1943. The Japanese had heavily defended the island and fought with their now expected fanatical resistance. Named 'Bloody Tarawa' the American 2nd Marine Division suffered over a period of seventy-six hours 3,407 casualties: 997 Marines and 30 sailors killed, 88 Marines missing and presumed dead, 2,233 Marines and 59 sailors wounded.[12]

Operation Flintlock was the campaign against the Marshall Islands and took place between January and February 1944. This operation involved the invasion of Kwajalein and Eniwetok Atolls. Using lessons learned from previous operations, the Marshall Islands were successfully taken from the Japanese by projecting joint air, sea and land forces with such overwhelming force that Japanese island fortresses quickly crumbled and fell.[13]

From this brief history it is possible to see that there was considerable experience available to the planners of Operation Overlord. We can also see that the problems of attempting a successful operation here were based on a set of distinct parameters that had to be dealt with. Whilst a huge bank of experience had been gained in amphibious operations, each one is different. To invade the coast of France would require combining experience on the similar elements of other operations already carried out but also to overcome new challenges relating specifically to this operation, a huge task that would require a lot of planning and preparation to achieve.

In June 1944 General Eisenhower, the supreme Commander of the Allied Expeditionary Force, wrote in his pre-D-Day message: 'The tide has turned! The free men of the world are marching together to victory!' The experience gained during the operations preceding D-Day would certainly contribute to that victory.

*Chapter Two*

# 1938: An Exercise in Invasion

The South Hams was no stranger to conflict. During the First World War many of its inhabitants had joined up to fight. War memorials in the villages and hamlets throughout the region are a testament to those who paid the ultimate sacrifice.

With its extensive coastline, South Devon has long had a maritime association. A major naval base and dockyard servicing the needs of the Royal Navy's ships has existed at Plymouth since 1691. Locally to the South Hams, The Britannia Royal Naval College at the nearby historic port of Dartmouth (the Pilgrim Fathers put in here on their way to America in 1620) has been the Royal Navy's officer training establishment since 1863.

Prior to the practice assault landings, taking place in 1944, the long shingle beach at Slapton Sands was in fact no stranger to amphibious landings, as it had previously been used for such purposes. In 1938 Germany had annexed Austria and also annexed the Sudetenland, then part of Czechoslovakia. With the growing ascendancy of the Nazi Party, war looked ever more likely. Re-armament was taking place and the armed forces of Great Britain were already training for a potential war with Nazi Germany.

In July 1938 a major combined arms amphibious landing exercise took place on Slapton Sands. The object of the exercise was to investigate the tactical and technical aspects of an approach from seaward landing of a force on an enemy coast. The assaulting force included the troopship HMT *Lancashire*[1] and the cargo ship SS *Clan MacAlister*[2] carrying motor transport, armoured vehicles and field guns.

The naval escort force consisted of destroyers and minesweepers as well as larger warships, including the Light Cruisers HMS *Sheffield*[3] and HMS *Southampton*[4]. The Aircraft Carrier HMS *Courageous*[5] provided the assaulting force with air cover and the battlecruiser HMS *Revenge*[6] helped provide heavier support with her 15" guns.

Planning for the exercise had started a month earlier and the assault troops taking part had commenced practicing embarking on the ships a fortnight before the landings.

Army units taking part in the exercise were the 2nd Battalion, The Lincolnshire Regiment; 1st Battalion, The Kings Own Scottish Borderers; 2nd Battalion, The Middlesex Regiment; 2nd Battalion, The East Yorkshire Regiment; 2nd Battalion, The Gloucestershire Regiment as well as detachments from the Royal Artillery, Royal Engineers, Royal Tank Corps, Royal Army Medical Corps and Military Police units[7].

The assaulting forces had embarked from Portsmouth on the *Lancashire* and the *Clan MacAlister* on Tuesday 4 July carrying the 'Eastland' forces that would assault the coast of 'Westland' or 'Wessex' at Slapton Sands. The beach assault force comprised of the 2nd Battalion, The Lincolnshire Regiment, and the 1st Battalion, The Kings Own Scottish Borderers who were part of the 9th Infantry Brigade, commanded by Brigadier Bernard Montgomery[8]. The 2nd Battalion, The East Yorkshire Regiment, part of the 8th Infantry Brigade, would also form part of the assault wave.

The assault force was to secure the beaches and then to secure the high ground surrounding the area opposite the beach. In all 2,300 troops were landed, the plan being to then re-embark the force back onto the ships.

During the night of Wednesday 6 July, a newspaper reporter located with the 'Eastland' defenders described the scene prior to the assault. 'When darkness fell at Slapton Sands tonight there seemed to be nothing unusual about this beautiful stretch of Devon coastline, but within a few hours it is anticipated that it will be one of the biggest combined exercises of the Navy, Army and Air Force which has ever taken place in the West-country.'

The beach landing was initially planned to be unopposed with an enemy reaction planned after the landing had taken place. This rather unrealistic scenario was however changed with the part of the defenders played by the 2nd Battalion of the Gloucester Regiment, who were deemed to consist entirely of a machine-gun force, having taken up positions on the high ground behind the beach. The basis of the assault however was still that the assaulting forces were much stronger then the defending forces. The plan also envisaged that the invaders would theoretically have to cater for heavier gunfire. The defenders were placed at high vantage points in the hinterland with observers keeping a watchful eye on the sea.

The landings commenced at 2.00 am on Wednesday 6 July on the northern part of the beach at Slapton Sands. Two companies of the 1st Battalion of the Kings Own Scottish Borderers landing on the left flank beach sector, codenamed 'Eclipse', and two companies of the 2nd Battalion of the Lincolnshire Regiment landing on the right flank beach sector codenamed 'Escapade'. One company of the 2nd Battalion of The East Yorkshire Regiment landed on the very northern end of Slapton beach near Matthews Point. Also the 2nd Battalion Middlesex Regiment landed later.

A local *Western Morning News* staff reporter described the assault: 'The actual landing which took place in the early hours of this morning was eerie. In the light of a pale moon the dim outlines of the troopship *Lancashire* and the transport *Clan MacAlister*, with her derricks raised in readiness, were seen a short distance from the shore.' The supporting naval force destroyers were lying close by to support the attack. *The Western Morning News* Reporter further describes the landings themselves, 'Then came the attack. Shortly after 2 o'clock boats began to come to shore and as they grounded troops with their rifles raised above their heads leaped out and splashed their way to the beach. Machine gun and rifle fire crackled from the interior.'

The scene of most of the landing was between Matthews Point and Strete Gate, where throughout the day the major coastal operations took place. A company of the East Yorkshire Regiment were the first ashore and they proceeded to block the main road east of Blackpool and secure the communications there. Simultaneously the troops of the 2nd Lincs landed and secured the Strete area and in the vicinity of Slapton Sands Hotel the Kings Own Scottish Borderers came ashore and made for the higher ground behind. The landing of the Middlesex Regiment completed the arrival of the troop forces.

As well as being located with the defending and assaulting forces, members of the press were also present on some of the naval force ships. With remarkable ingenuity one reporter from *The Western Morning News* on the cruiser HMS *Sheffield*, managed to ensure his story reached the office to be included in the next day's paper. By hitching a ride in the ships catapult-launched aircraft he managed to drop his report on the village of Strete, where a surprised bystander, who had observed the package fall from the aircraft, picked it up and read the instructions 'From HMS *Sheffield* – will finder please immediately phone Plymouth 2313, asking them to collect this envelope' written on the package. With commendable promptitude, the bystander took the package to the Post Office at Strete where Miss I. Wallis, following the instructions, contacted *The Western Morning News*. The newspaper picked up the copy and was able to print the story: 'Dropped from the skies!'

After landing, The East Yorkshires captured a dispatch rider of the Gloucestershire Regiment (the defenders) before he was able to fire a Very light as warning and a platoon of the KOSBs also managed to capture all except one of a Gloucestershire machine-gun section. The man who escaped was able to give information however and the Borderers later found the road blocked and were surprised by an NCO and troops attached to Gloucestershire trucks. By daybreak 'Eastland' had obtained command of the beach but their operations were considerably hampered by aircraft which roared overhead. Gradually things began to take shape. Food, equipment, water, supplies and hundreds of tins of petrol were brought ashore. Then the sappers got busy laying tracks for the heavier vehicles. Machine-gun carriers, transport lorries and small whippet tanks were slung over the side of the *Clan McAlister* on to the lighters waiting in readiness. The assault troops then proceeded to advance into the interior and despite opposition by the Gloucestershire's they succeeded in securing and holding an area of about 1½ miles in width stretching inland from a five-mile coastline. Wessex aircraft made simulated attacks on the landing beaches in the afternoon. The landing forces were eventually ordered to withdraw with a message transmitted to the Ninth Infantry Brigade assault forces 'Expedition to withdraw. Arrange with G.S.2 to re-embark personnel during darkness 6–7. Transport and stores, if necessary to be destroyed on the beach'.

By 6 o'clock the sky had clouded over and an hour later rain was falling in torrents. The sea developed a considerable swell. Shortly before 9 o'clock the assault troops had returned to the beach in readiness for re-embarkation. The 2nd Battalion Middlesex Regiment began to re-embark, and at about this time the KOSBs and Lincolnshires began to thin out their positions, the East Yorkshires occupying the high ground near Strete to cover their withdrawal. The weather also conspired to be the enemy of the assaulting force. On Wednesday 7 July the plan to re-embark the landing forces had to be abandoned. A strong gale had blown up with blinding rain. It became obvious that to attempt further re-embarkation would be too dangerous and risk of injury and possible loss of life was too great. Some troops from the Middlesex Regiment had managed to be safely re-embarked but 1000 of the troops, including 50 officers and 100 naval ratings still on shore were forced to march five miles in the gale and blinding rain to shelter at the Britannia Royal Naval College at Dartmouth.

Arrangements were made to accommodate them there. Many of the men were weary and soaked to the skin as a result of taking part in the exercise and having had to march the five miles to the college in the pouring rain. *The Western Morning News* reported on Friday 8 July 'Throughout the night the troops soaked with rain filed through the doors of the college for the first real shelter they had had for many hours. All available space was used to accommodate them'. The next day the naval ratings were re-embarked onto their ships from Dartmouth and the Army personnel transported back to their bases by lorry.

So ended the first assault landing at Slapton Sands. Differing conclusions were reached as a result of the practice assault. It was concluded that 'in the face of considerable opposition on the shore it would be very improbable that a landing without great loss of life could be affected on a coastline such as this.'[9]

With regard to the involvement of aircraft, it was concluded that aircraft would play an important part in repulsing such an invasion. Whilst fire would be directed on them by naval ships, the absence of anti-aircraft guns on the beach in the early stages of the landing would make the task of the aircraft a comparatively easy one.

The tactical and technical aspects of an approach from the sea and the handling of a force on a hostile coast were closely examined. The whole exercise was considered to have been 'an interesting one and most useful to the authorities of the Army, Navy and Air Force[10]. There was also considerable criticism however. It was stated that it could hardly be conceivable that the number of the attacking 'Eastland' forces could have begun their operations without being observed and a considerable enemy force gathered to 'give them a warm welcome'.

Victory in the mock war was deemed to have gone to the defending forces where, if real warfare had prevailed, would have played havoc with the assaulting troops if actual re-embarkation had had to take place.

The choice of using a lightly opposed defender scenario was also criticised. It was deemed that 'an opposed landing would have been impossible, so the scenario that was used was where watcher on shore would give alarm of the enemy landings in time for the surrounding high ground to be occupied.' It was noted however 'in this exercise the idea of a potential race for the heights did not appear very much in evidence'.[11]

General criticism was also made about the difficulty of the exercise: 'Would not the exercise have been richer in experience gained and lessons learned and therefore made more worthwhile, if conditions had been deliberately made harder?'[12]

Unbeknown to those taking part in the 1938 exercise there were a number of parallels with the operation that would happen just over six years later on the beaches of Normandy in June 1944. In July 1938, the assault force had to contend with a strong southwesterly gale prior to the scheduled assault. This caused considerable problems with the planned landings and seasickness amongst the assault troops, who were forced to endure seventeen hours at sea prior to landing. The same would occur on 5 June 1944, when cloudy skies, rain and heavy seas caused the assault to be postponed for twenty-four hours. Of the regiments taking part in 1938, the 1st Battalion of the Kings Own Scottish Borderers, the 2nd Battalion of the Lincolnshire Regiment, 2nd Battalion, The Middlesex Regiment and 2nd Battalion, The East Yorkshire Regiment (The Duke of York's Own) would once again land together as part of the 3rd Infantry Division on Sword Beach on 6 June 1944. The defenders at Slapton Sands in 1938, 2nd Battalion the Gloucestershire Regiment would come ashore at Gold Beach on 6th June, D-Day, as part of 56th Brigade. Some of the ships taking part in the 1938 exercise would also go on to play their part in the Normandy landings. The *Lancashire* would also be present off Juno Beach on 6 June 1944, acting as a commodore ship. By late 1943 the battlecruiser HMS *Revenge* had been withdrawn from operational service due to being in poor condition, and reduced to reserve status, initially serving as a stoker's training ship. However, Prime Minister Winston Churchill stated that this venerable battleship should be put to better use. Churchill embarked on *Revenge* to sail to Malta, as a leg of the journey to the Tehran Conference in November 1943. But by September 1944 the ship was in very poor condition and had been decommissioned and placed in reserve. Her main armament of 15"/42 Mark I guns were removed to provide spare guns for the battleships *Ramillies* and *Warspite*, as well as the monitor HMS *Roberts* which were to be vital during the bombardment of the beaches of Normandy during Operation Overlord.

Considering historical data was available from actual amphibious assault landings carried out in anger in previous conflicts, the practice assault at Slapton Sands in 1938 seems rather amateurish and unrealistic (the exercise scenario planned to evacuate only twenty wounded cases). An extensive military Manual of Combined Operations[13] was also available in 1938. This defined in great detail how a combined arms amphibious assault should be organised and take place. Looking at the contents however shows how out of date it really was. A table showed details of Motor Landing Craft, Motor Lighters and Horse boats that were available for use in amphibious landings. The types of craft listed include 'X' Lighters, which are detailed as being capable of carrying 500 men, four 18-pdr guns and forty horses, or eleven 18-pdr guns. This type of craft is detailed as having been used during the war of 1914–18 and that there were few now available. Another type of craft listed is the Horse boat (1915 design). The more modern Motor Landing Craft (No. 10 type) was a more flexible craft and could carry men, mechanised vehicles, artillery and light tanks. It was also detailed as being capable of carrying twelve horses and twelve men. The emphasis on the capability to transport horses shows how ill-prepared the British Armed Forces were when only a year later in 1939 war broke out. It also perhaps highlights the progress made in both the technology and tactics of amphibious assaults by the time the Normandy Landings occurred in June 1944.

The exercise was held in a very public manner. Among those who watched the landings were the Earl of Cork and Orrery (Commander-in-chief, Portsmouth), Viscount Gort VC Chief of the Imperial General Staff, and General A.F. Wavell GOC Southern Command.

The object of the exercise had been publicly stated as having been to investigate the tactical and technical aspects of an approach from the sea and the landing of a force on an enemy coast. It must have also acted as a strong demonstration of the country's armed forces to the British public and also to the country's enemies.

The beaches at Slapton Sands had played a key part in providing the ability to practice and learn vital lessons in relation to a beach assault. Six years later, the troops would be back and once more Slapton sands would play a vital part as an assault beach training area.

*Chapter Three*

# The South Hams: An Area Overview

This area of South Devon known as the South Hams is one of the most beautiful and peaceful parts of the United Kingdom. It has a distinctive landscape, featuring rolling hills with high-banked lanes bordering small fields. Small woods and copses punctuate the landscape. Long rivers with estuaries are also a feature of this area with rivers such as the Dart and the Erme providing not only excellent fishing but also places to cruise and enjoy the magnificent views. The rocky coastline with interspaced shingle and sandy beaches is particularly spectacular. Small farms run by long-standing farming families form a major part of the local economy. In the summer months, thousands of tourists flock to South Devon and enjoy the scenery, the beaches, the ancient historical towns and the many attractions. Not far inland the wild landscape of Dartmoor is easily accessible.

Whilst the landscape has remained largely unchanged, today the communities that now inhabit the area have changed considerably. In 1943 the community was made up largely of local families that had lived in the area, many for generations. Local names predominated with Trants, Tuckers, Wills, and many more forming a network of local families. Visitors from far away as London came to enjoy the excellent hunting, shooting and fishing. The local Devon accent predominated.

The village communities were largely self-sufficient with bakeries, shops, schools, farriers, blacksmiths and many other business providing goods and services to the community. What could not be provided locally could mostly be found in the nearby market towns of Dartmouth, Kingsbridge and Totnes.

There was no mains water or electricity available to most of the farms and houses in the area. Water was provided from springs and wells (taps were located around villages). Some electricity was provided by generators, but most lighting was provided using oil lamps.

In November 1943, as part of the process of establishing the suitability of the area for assault training, a detailed study was carried out by the Inter-

Departmental Committee on Combined Training Areas. The Committee produced a report[1] on the area, which provides a detailed description of the area at that time.

It reported that most local business were geared to agriculture. The area was recognised as being of very considerable importance for food with the land being above average fertility. The area had 20,200 acres of good quality agricultural land, of which fifty per cent was under the plough. The crops grown in 1943 included 6,200 acres of corn, 600 acres of potatoes, 1,560 acres of root crop and temporary grass. Livestock as of the 4 June 1943 included 1,620 dairy cows, 3,500 other cattle, 11,000 sheep, 850 pigs, 16,000 poultry, and 580 horses.

The area was described as being of an exceedingly enclosed nature with the fields on average less than six acres in extent, of which there were at least 2,500 separate fields in number. The majority of these fields were enclosed by typical Devon 'banked hedges' or bounded by narrow sunken lanes, in many places twenty feet deep.

Owing to the exceptionally undulating nature of the country, the quality of the land varied considerably; the pasture, from deep meadow land to rough hill grazing, and the arable land comprising of noted barley land to recently reclaimed waste land. At least eighty per cent of area was described as being good quality agricultural land worth approx £40 per acre in the open market at that time.

Apart from small holdings (not exceeding five acres in extent) which were estimated to number thirty, 150 individual farms were cottage type dwellings with ten or twenty acres and poor buildings. The majority averaged about seventy-five acres and consisted of stone houses and buildings. They were for the most part occupied by tenant farmers who employed little labour apart from their own families. Now in wartime they also employed Land Girls.

An estimate of the head of stock that would be affected by assault training (based on information obtained from the Lands Commissioner) was given as: 3,500 cattle (which included approx. 1,200 dairy cows), 7,500 sheep and 600 pigs.

The approximate number of the civilian population in each parish affected comprised: Blackawton (550), East Allington (390), Strete (320), Slapton (450). The total population of Torcross, Beeson, Stokenham, Chillington and Sherford, was estimated to be in the region of 900. As well as those entire parishes lying entirely inside the evacuation area some other parishes were also included: Halwell (14%), Woodleigh (4%), Stoke Fleming (30%), Buckland-tout-Saints (20%), Sherford (2%), and Stokenham (25%). The inhabitants of the above were estimated to be 140.

The area was recognised by the Ministry of Works as having a number of 'properties of character' as well as being 'places of historic interest'. These were detailed as East Allington Church, Blackawton Church, Slapton Church, Stokenham Church, Sherford Church, Keynedon House, Sherford, and the Chantry and Poole House at Slapton.

Additionally there were some substantial private country residences in area:

Fallapit House, East Allington
Sheplegh Court, Blackawton
Stokeley House, Stokenham
Bowden House, Stoke Fleming
Asherne, Strete
Prospect House, Slapton
Blackpool Cottage, Stoke Fleming (the residence of Major Newbury, the grounds of which contained a rare collection of tropical plants)
Torcross Hotel
Widdicombe House, Torcross
Grey Homes (private hotel at Torcross)
Coleridge House, near Chillington

The area also contained six inns, various small retail premises, and a number of superior cottage-type dwellings. It was estimated that the 1939 aggregate rental values of all the premises in area excluding land would exceed £25,000 per annum.

At that time the only military installations in the area consisted of an Air Ministry WT station (at Strete), and anti-aircraft coastal defence measures and anti-invasion works. The personnel involved in manning these installations occupied Fallapit House near East Allington, and Stokeley House near Stokenham.

The public services consisted of electricity supplied by the Borough of Torquay, a bulk supply being carried by an overhead 33,000-volt cable from Totnes to Kingsbridge, whence it was distributed by an 11,000-volt overhead line running via Stokenham, Slapton, Strete and Stoke Fleming to Dartmouth, and thence back to Totnes.

The water supply was provided by the Kingsbridge and Salcombe Water Boards. A 5-inch main fed a 50,000 gallon reservoir at Sherford Cross from which the air ministry had run a 4-inch pipeline to their station at Prawle, approximately eleven miles south. All the villages in the area depended on springs and wells.

The minor roads consisted mostly of sunken lanes thickly interspersed. The coast route ran from Dartmouth to Kingsbridge via the beach at Slapton Sands.

The nearest railway was the Totnes-South Brent-Kingsbridge branch of the Great Western Railway.

A major BBC radio transmitting station existed at nearby Start Point. This transmitter was designed and built in 1939. It was equipped with two transmitters. The BBC Forces Programme was transmitted from here. Another local link to D-Day exists with this transmitter, as shortly after D-Day one of the transmitters which had been upgraded started transmitting the new Allied Expeditionary Forces Programme (AEFP) to the troops in Europe. Start Point was the only transmitter that transmitted the AEF programme from the UK and as the allies advance progressed, relay stations were used to transmit the programme to France and Germany. The service continued until the cessation of hostilities in Europe

An Air Ministry WT station also existed at nearby Prawle[2]. This was the site of a Chain Home radar station, Chain Home Low station. It was commissioned in January 1939 to provide early warning of enemy aircraft approaching industrial areas in Bristol and South Wales.

Certainly similarities do exist between the South Hams and the Normandy beaches, as well as the Normandy hinterland beyond. The geographical similarities, if not deliberate, were certainly advantageous in many ways.

During my research I have not discovered any direct reference to the Slapton Sands area being selected for training the American Forces that would land at the Utah and Omaha Beaches.

*Chapter Four*

# 1940–1942: Invasion Beach for Real and the War in the Air

In 1939 the shadow of war fell on The South Hams. With the fall of France in 1940 and an imminent invasion by the Germans expected, extensive beach defences were put in place to prevent assault from the Sea. The South Devon beaches, including the beach at Slapton Sands, were heavily mined, and barbed wire defences and latticed scaffolding[1] beach defences had been erected.

In July 1940, the 11th Battalion, Durham Light Infantry took over the defence of the South Hams from 8th Battalion, Royal Northumberland Fusiliers. Part of the 70th Infantry Brigade comprising the 11th Battalion DLI, the 10th Battalion DLI and 1st Battalion Tyneside Scottish, 11 DLI had been sent to France as part of the British Expeditionary Force and took part in the Battle of France in 1940. Having been evacuated via the beaches of Dunkirk on 31 May 1940, they were now positioned to defend the Slapton Sands area. The battalion had fought hard during the actions in France. The strength of 11th DLI when it left for France to join the BEF on 24 April 1940 was 24 officers and 628 men. It returned with only 12 officers and 384 men. The Brigade had to cover a front from the River Yealm in the south to the River Exe in the north. Clear instructions were issued to all troops that in the event of an invasion, all positions were to be held to the last man, and there would be no withdrawal. The 1st Battalion Tyneside Scottish held the line from Newton Ferrers to Start Point. The 11th DLI covered the area from Start Point to Dartmouth with the 10th DLI responsible for the stretch of coast from Shaldon to Dawlish. Three of the battalions companies were allocated positions around the Slapton area, B Company at Torcross, C Company at Slapton and D Company at Strete. The Battalion HQ and HQ Company were based at Stanborough Brake near Halwell. Work to build invasion defences started during July and went on through August and the first half of September. The tasks to be carried out as a priority included digging weapon pits and LMG posts, making camouflage arrangements to cover activity, improving fields of fire, wiring posts, constructing command posts, digging slit trenches near billets, preparing alternative positions, building of road blocks, setting up anti-tank obstacles, building section posts, erecting anti-aircraft pylons on the Torcross-Strete road (this consisted of concrete piping, two feet in diameter and fourteen feet high, at about five yard intervals) and building pillboxes.

As well as working hard on building defences, the battalion also manned road blocks. The beach road from the Torcross-Strete road was closed between 22:00 hours and 05:00 hours each day. At night, all vehicles approaching road blocks were stopped. All platoons mounted anti-aircraft Bren guns during the day, and took turns in occupying the various defence posts. Joint exercises were held and liaison maintained with the LDV (Local Defence Volunteers, subsequently the Home Guard) who were recognised as being valuable sources of local information. Companies stood-to everyday at first and last light.

Beach patrols were carried out from 23:00 hours to 03:00 hours each night, or from time to time as dictated by the Intelligence Officer. These patrols consisted of an NCO and four men, each with a loaded rifle and twenty rounds, and with bayonet fixed. The patrols were expected to move in tactical formation and had specific orders to: check isolated boats which were not to be fired on unless they clearly contained enemy (they were to be checked by a small armed party, covered by an LMG ready to fire if necessary); observe for signals of distress, or signals from Naval Coastal Patrols; watch for signs of vessels approaching the shore (if this occurred they were to alert colleagues by means of Very lights, posts seeing them being required to inform HQ immediately. This would also be the signal for all Posts to be 100% manned); deal with any suspicious movement of persons on the beach (pending the establishment of a curfew); searching houses along the beach and in the neighbourhood.

Initially the battalion had lacked weapons and manpower, having lost plenty of both in France. In one instance an officer was nearly put on a charge by the Brigade Commander when he saw that he was not wearing a revolver. It was only when it was explained that it was 'not his turn to wear the revolver', as there was only one between six officers that the Brigadier relented[2].

The battalion was slowly made back up to strength during the period that they were in the South Hams. Losses in weapons were made up and Lewis, Maxim, Hotchkiss and Vickers machine guns were eventually issued to the various companies. Transport, other arms and equipment also began to arrive rapidly to meet the Brigade's requirements. During August a demonstration of a Flame Trap device[3] was held at Strete – attended by Admiral Naismith (Senior Officer Commanding Plymouth) and other senior officers from Southern Command. After the trial, the Flame Trap was installed on the road leading inland from the beach to Strete. Also during August, work continued on the defences, and pillboxes were completed at Torcross, Slapton and Strete. As well as the Flame Trap, additional fixed equipment was added to bolster the beach defences. A 6-inch mortar[4] was installed at Strete with a second positioned at Torcross. A searchlight was positioned at Torcross for the purpose of illuminating the beach. Firing practice was carried out on the ranges set up at Strete, with every man completing a course on the rifle, light machine gun and grenade. In addition, firing practice was carried out on the 2-inch mortar, anti-tank rifle, and Maxim and Vickers guns. An additional military presence was also added in September when an RAF West wireless telegraphy security station was established at Strete Gate. In September an 'Air Spray' demonstration took place at Slapton. This was to show what a low-altitude chemical spray attack would be like. Various units, including a company of 2nd Gloucesters, two companies of 11th DLI, one company of 1st Tyneside Scottish, and a detachment from Brigade HQ were submitted to the spray, and instructed by Colonel Ware, the commanding officer of 11th DLI[5].

On 7 September 1940 across the country the dreaded invasion appeared to have started. At 21:25 hours the code-word 'Cromwell', indicating 'invasion imminent', was received at Brigade Headquarters and forwarded to units within the sub-area. Across the country as well as at Slapton Sands, the defenders braced for the long expected German Invasion.

During the period of the Cromwell alert, Home Guard units were mobilised and manned their pillboxes. All flyable training aircraft that weren't fighters were converted into bombers. Police rounded up trainee pilots, some barely able to fly, from pubs, dance halls and cinemas, and as they reported back to their airfields they were shocked to see bombs being loaded onto their flimsy training aircraft. More than half of Bomber Command's medium bombers stood by to support Home Forces. Some church bells were sounded: the signal that enemy troops were in the area. Several East Anglian bridges were blown up by the Royal Engineers and there were more serious consequences when three Guards officers were killed in Lincolnshire when their vehicle went over a newly laid mine as they rushed back to their posts. Whilst eventually being recognised as a false alarm for the defenders of Slapton Sands, at the time for the men of the 11th DLI it had been very real. When the alarm was sounded by battalion headquarters, troops rushed out to man the defensive positions. Part of the motley array of transport provided for the DLI included several motor cycles, two motor cycle and side-car combinations, a wedding car impressed from the village, two buses and two trucks. Racing out through the gates of the billet, the wedding car got stuck and turmoil ensued. The men raced to positions on Slapton Sands and an officer present at the time, 2nd Lieutenant Kenneth Johnstone commented 'If Hitler had seen us, I'm sure he would have had a good laugh.' Subsequent practice improved response and eventually the troops were able to deploy to the beach within ten minutes.

The remainder of the time spent at Slapton Sands was quiet apart from 9 September 1940 when, after a quiet night, at 08:30 hours a dog exploded a land mine on Slapton Beach.

While 11 DLI were stationed in the Slapton area, they worked hard defending as well as building defences. During the summer of 1940 there was a record spell of fine weather, which assisted the work programme and also gave a welcome opportunity for frequent bathing parties. Home and local leave passes were issued. When on short local leave, the 'liberty' truck took men from the camps to nearby villages for an evening out – focused, of course, on the local public houses. The Orderly Sergeant mounted the truck full of men and gave them all a most solemn warning before they set off about the strength of the local brew, which of course was 'scrumpy' or rough cider. These were largely hard manual workers from the industrial northeast, used to drinking beer in large quantities, and they did not take too kindly to what they regarded as a 'schoolboy lecture' on the dangers of alcohol.

The party was picked up at 10:30 later that evening. When the truck drew into the village for the pickup of the libertymen, a long line of khaki–clad bodies stretched out along the grass verge outside one of the public houses, surrounded by amused locals. With the odd exception, the troops had all ignored the sergeant's warning, and had also ignored the fact that the locals were drinking half-pints of scrumpy, very slowly. After consuming three or four pints each, speedily, they had succumbed to the surprising alcoholic strength of this native brew and had been carried outside into the fresh air to await their transport, much to the amusement of the local worthies.[6] Like many that have had a similar experience with the strong local cider, it was one that was taken on board and not repeated so enthusiastically again!

In mid-September 11 DLI handed over to the 2nd Battalion of the Gloucester Regiment. The 70th Infantry Brigade was to be sent to Iceland where it took over from the Royal Regiment of Canada. At the end of 1941 the 11th DLI returned home to the UK, the defence of Iceland having become an American responsibility. On 12 June 1944, six days after the initial D-Day landings, the 11th DLI would come ashore as part of 70th Infantry Brigade.

The time spent by the DLI at Slapton Sands had been valuable. Not only had they been in place to defend the area, they had completed many of the beach defences. These beach defences were once again to play a part in early 1944 where they provided defences set-up for the attacking assault troops as well as targets for the naval bombardments supporting the practice assaults.

With the threat of invasion fading, the effects of the war in the air now began to be felt on the South Hams. The Luftwaffe now became the primary arm of aggression over Great Britain. In South Devon one of the initial incidents was related to a raid on the city of Plymouth. On 27 November 1940 a bomb was dropped on Torcross.[7] On this day a major attack on Plymouth had taken place. Units of Luftflotte 3 flying from airfields in occupied France had attacked Devonport dockyard and also bombed targets in the north and northwest parts of the town. The attacks took place between 18.30 and 02.10 by 112 aircraft that dropped a mixture of high explosive and incendiary bombs[8]. The bomb dropped at Torcross destroyed buildings, including Harwoods shop [9]. Luckily nobody was killed.

The area continued to feel the effects of the air war. Hannafords butchers at Torcross suffered a near miss in 1942 causing damage to a building in the yard at the rear of the premises. During 1942 and 1943 the Luftwaffe carried out a series of raids that became known as 'Tip and Run' raids. Specially trained pilots flying Focke Wulf Fw 190 fighter bombers ranged over the area attacking targets of opportunity. The idea of the attacks was to target anything that would terrorise the British public, 'Trains, motor buses, gatherings of people, herds of cattle and sheep, etc' were specifically mentioned as legitimate targets[10].

The whole of the local area suffered from these attacks, including the towns of Torquay, Exmouth, Salcombe and Kingsbridge, where a number of people were killed. Random attacks were also made with German aircraft strafing the villages of Torcross and Slapton.

On 26 July 1942 at 17.00, two Focke Wulf Fw190 aircraft of 10/*JG 2* took off to attack targets of opportunity around the South Devon coast in the Start Point area. At 17.50 they bombed what they believed to be Torcross. In fact they had attacked the small village of Beesands. The bombs exploded causing a tragic loss of life. 4-year-old Mary Lamble, 23-year-old May Bullen, her 14-month-old son Brian Bullen, and 54-year-old auxiliary coastguard Cornelius Warth were amongst those killed. Two-year-old John Nile, the son of Able Seaman John Henry Nile., and Doris Nile were also killed.[11]

On 26 January 1943, eight Fw 190 fighter bombers of 10/*JG 2* took off at 15:15 to attack Kingsbridge. The aircraft were however unable to attack Kingsbridge, due to the weather, so diverted to their secondary target – Loddiswell. The aircraft attacked, machine gunning and dropping their bombs, but again they had misidentified their target. It was in fact the village of Aveton Gifford, seven miles from Slapton. Seven bombs were dropped on the village with direct hits made on the Rectory and on St Andrews Church, severely damaging it. Of the 110 houses in the village only five were undamaged. Twenty villagers were injured, three seriously[12] and five-year-old Sonia Weeks, the daughter of Petty Officer Sydney and Nellie Weeks, was killed.

One of the attackers was shot down over Start Bay after the attack. Fw Karl Blase, an experienced pilot, was shot down by a Hawker Typhoon piloted by 266 Squadron pilot Fg Off Clive Bell.

The impact of the Tip and Run raids had a direct impact on Strete on 23 March 1943. Five aircraft of II/*SKG* 10 attacked the nearby town of

Dartmouth. The aircraft came under fire from defending anti–aircraft guns and the FW 190A-5 aircraft flown by Oblt Oswald Laumann was hit and smoke began to pour from his engine. The aircraft crashed at 19:15 on the outskirts of Strete killing the pilot, and was witnessed by local people. Local resident Pam Wills who was a child at the time remembered hearing the air raid sirens being sounded in Dartmouth and hiding under a table that had been specially placed as a shelter in an alcove for such occasions[13]. Another local resident – Ken Parnell, who was a schoolboy at the time, also remembers hearing the aircraft crash and rushing to the scene to see it with its nose in the hedge and burning fiercely. Like many small boys at the time Ken was looking for souvenirs, but was quickly ordered away once the local special constable appeared[14].

The aircraft had broken into three sections. Amongst the effects of the pilot found were his identity tag and two coins, one German and one Polish. Laumann was the Gruppen Adjutant of II/*SKG* 10 and this was believed to be his first operational flight. Born in Berlin in 1915, 28–year–old Laumann held a doctorate in law. He was buried at Weston Mill Cemetery in Plymouth but later exhumed along with other German casualties and reburied at Cannock Chase German Military Cemetery. Laumann's family claimed his remains in June 1962, and he was again reburied at the Friedhof Heerdt in Düsseldorf.

The aircraft site was subject to an investigation in later years by the Devon Aircraft Research and Recovery Team, but little evidence of the crash was found. Amazingly, some of Laumann's personal remains turned up many years later and included parts of his burnt uniform insignia and the Polish coin! These are now in the possession of a private collector.[15]

The effects of these raids, as might be expected, directly affected RAF units in the area. Not only were they required to make defensive air patrols of the area and intercept raids when they took place, a variety of other tasks were carried out by the RAF. One of these was to provide Air Sea Rescue cover. No 276 Squadron was formed at Harrowbeer on 21 October 1941, from detachments of air sea rescue aircraft at Harrowbeer, Roborough, Warmwell, Perranporth and Fairwood Common. Its area of operations covered the western end of the English Channel and the Bristol Channel. Avro Anson Westland Lysander aircraft were used for spotting ditched planes and could drop dinghies and supplies to survivors in the water. Amphibious Westland Walrus aircraft could then be used for picking up the ditched crews.

An unusual event happened off Slapton Sands on 24 August 1942. Westland Lysander T1696/AQ-H of 276 Squadron was on a training flight flown by Royal Canadian Air Force Pilot Officer Jack Ernst, with crewman AC2 Stuart Fleet. The aircraft disappeared and was eventually reported as missing. Rumours circulated that Jack Ernst had defected, the rationale for this apparently being his Germanic surname. It is known that on this date four fighter bomber aircraft from 10/JG 26 had taken off from Caen to perform an armed reconnaissance in the vicinity of Start Point. The aircraft dropped bombs on Dartmouth and on the return journey recorded contact with two Spitfires and a Lysander but made no claims. It seems likely that the Lysander they met was that being flown by Jack Ernst. As the German pilots had made no claim of damage of shooting down any of the aircraft they had encountered. Pilot Officer Ernst may have crashed perhaps whilst taking evasive action. No trace of either Jack Ernst or of Stuart Fleet has ever been found[16]. Both men are recorded on the Runnymede Memorial[17].

By 1943 the people and the defenders of the South Hams were no strangers to war and the tragedy it brings. But they were about to become much more closely involved than they could ever have imagined.

*Chapter Five*

# Selection of Training Areas

Training is a vital part of the success of any military operation. The key to training is land. Space where troops can manoeuvre, fire weapons and exercise, not only in safety for themselves, but also where the general public will not be at risk and cannot interfere.

Traditionally in Great Britain military training has been carried out on land owned by the Ministry of Defence or its predecessor the War Office. These training areas are usually located in the more remote areas of the country.

In 1939 with the declaration of war against Germany on Monday 3 September came the realisation that there would be a need to train thousands of troops. This in turn would require additional training facilities and land. As a result land was requisitioned for this purpose. The need to train had to be carefully weighed against the need to use all viable land for food and livestock production, to help the country become as self-sufficient as possible. This provided a conflict between those responsible for food production and those responsible for training the Armed Forces. Where possible, unproductive land with low populations was chosen for training areas. The plan was to utilise this land for the duration of the war, then hand it back once it was no longer required.

As well as using existing training areas, many new training areas were set up. Woods, moorland, downland and heath became training areas. Chalk pits and quarries rifle ranges. Beaches were used to fire weapons out to sea.

Whilst these worked well for training in land warfare, in 1943 there was little existing provision for large areas of land to practice beach assault landings. For the forthcoming assault on Nazi-held Europe, large areas of beach would be required to practice assault landings.

The decision to invade mainland Europe had been formally made at the Casablanca Conference during 14–24 January 1943 between US President

Franklin D. Roosevelt and British Prime Minister Winston Churchill (the Soviet Premier Joseph Stalin had received an invitation, but was unable to attend due to the Red Army being engaged in a major offensive).

Within the United Kingdom at this time, whilst some beach locations were available for combined arms training, many of the coastal training areas were utilised as bombing and gunnery ranges for the RAF. Most coastal areas on the south and east coasts of the country had also been fortified against potential German invasion, by laying mines and erecting anti-invasion defences.

For Operation Overlord responsibility for the coordination of service requirements for assault training was the responsibility of the Admiralty.

Operation Overlord would involve the formation and training of five Naval Assault Forces, each of which would be able to lift approximately one division at assault scales. Lift was also to be provided for assault Commandos.

One of the most important requirements would be practice with live ammunition in supporting the landing and subsequent operations of troops using fire support. Most types of landing craft, in addition to support craft and destroyers, would be exercised in providing this support as well as providing the actual landing capability for the assault troops. In addition the various flotillas and groups of landing craft which comprised the Naval Assault Force would require experience in synchronising landings with air support and generally the requirements for all of the three services would need to be catered for.

The Admiralty would also be responsible for undertaking the task of selecting suitable areas, in consultation with the War Office, the Air Ministry and the Chief of Combined Services. For that purpose a special committee was formed: the Assault Training Area Selection committee (ATASC) and chaired by Captain R.J.L. Phillips RN.

The terms of reference of the committee were:

A. To examine and make proposals to provide areas for Combined Assault Training for the special purposes required by COSSAC[1]
B. To obtain all necessary information for the consideration and coordination of these proposals, affecting liaison with such other Government Departments as may be deemed necessary.
C. To recommend suitable sites and report.

The Admiralty were to select and arrange a reconnaissance of possible areas to determine the precise locations of the potential beach assault training areas immediately required.

In June 1943 there was in existence only one close support range on the south coast. This was the Needles range, which had been developed towards the close of 1942 and had been almost in constant use ever since. This range however was deemed far too small and its landing beaches too exposed, to render it suitable for the task of training for the scale of assault training now required. New areas were required, and the initial definition of requirements was defined as:

1. Two areas within 30 miles of Milford Haven
2. One area between Plymouth and Falmouth
3. One area between Dartmouth and Prawle Point
4. Two areas between Portland and the Needles
5. One area between Yarmouth and Harwich
6. One area between Bridlington and Spurn Point
7. Two areas in the Rosyth Command

This would ideally provide two practice areas for the use of each assault force. The principal reason for requesting two areas lay in the fact that the bulk of their training would necessarily take place during the winter and early spring. This being so, the weather would play a governing part in the rate at which training could be completed. By having two areas for each Naval Assault Force, it was hoped that there would be a landing beach sheltered from a different direction to the other, thereby reducing the number of days in which exercises had to be suspended due to weather.

It was also considered doubtful that a single training area would suffice for a complete Naval Assault Force. Each area needed to be approximately the right size for exercising a landing on a battalion scale, although by accepting somewhat unrealistic conditions, it would probably be possible to exercise a Brigade-size landing group. As each Assault Force included units needed for no less than six battalion landings, it was appreciated that an attempt to train the entire force in one area, except perhaps during the summer months, was likely to present considerable difficulties.

There was also a further consideration of the distance of the areas from the ports at which the units requiring training were based. Many of these units were small and required to be landed by what was considered relatively unseaworthy landing craft, and experience had shown that it was very difficult to arrange exercises which involved making a sea passage for these types of vessels of any length.

The requirement, it was believed, would meet the future needs of United States troops for areas of this type, with the assumption that they would be accorded the use of the site at Woolacombe (Appledore)[2]. No further requests were anticipated for the provision of training for US Forces.

At this stage no specific date requirement was set, as this depended on the progress made with the formation of the Naval Assault Forces, which were not yet in place.

The requirements of each training area were summarised as:

1. Each should have a sea frontage of from 2 and a half to 3 nautical miles, and should extend at least 5,000 and preferably 8,000 yards inland.
2. Each area must include at least one beach suitable for landing at most states of the tide, not less than 500 yards long and if possible 1,000 yards.
3. The seaward approaches to the landing beaches should be comparatively easy.
4. The areas should be sparsely inhabited and it is important that arrangements for clearing them to permit practice firing should be capable of being made at twelve hours notice. (Longer notice than this is particularly undesirable on account of the difficulty of forecasting weather conditions in practices of the nature visualised).
5. It is essential that the seaward approaches to the areas should be swept and that beach mines should be cleared from the landing beaches[3].

The initial areas selected as possible locations were:

Two areas within 30 miles of Milford Haven.
Length of beach 12,400 yards. Depth inland 8,000 yards.
This comprised of two areas joined in one stretch.

Plymouth and Falmouth.
The coast of Veryan Bay from Hartriza Point to Hemmick Beach.
Length of beach 6,000 yards. Depth inland 7,100 yards.

Dartmouth and Prawle Point.
The coast Torcross to Strete.
Length of beach 5,100 yards. Depth inland 7,500 yards.

Portland and Needles.
The coast of Worbarrow and Kimmeridge Bay.
Length of beach 6,000 yards. Depth inland 6,500 yards.

The coast of Studland Bay
Length of beach 4,400 yards. Depth inland 8,000 yards.

Yarmouth and Harwich.

The coast north of Dunwich.
The length of beach 4,700 yards. Depth inland 5,400 yards.
[This was part of an existing Battle Training Area]

Bridlington and Spurn.
Length of beach 6,000 yards. Depth inland 7,500 yards.

Rosyth Command.

Scotland, Culbin Sands.
Length of beach 7,500 yards. Depth inland 5,000 yards.

Scotland, Hopeman coast.
Length of beach 6,000 yards. Depth inland 7,000 yards

One other possible area in Scotland at Sinclair Bay.
Length of beach 6,000 yards. Depth inland 8,000 yards.

The first meeting of the Assault Training Area Selection committee took place on Thursday 6 July 1943 at 11:30, at the Admiralty in London. The initial focus of the committee was to obtain a statement of requirements for a typical assault training area and the creation of a general policy for drawing up a programme of action. A list of dates training areas would be required was made available and ranged from the beginning of October to the end of December 1943. The Slapton Area was listed as being required by November 1943, a mere four months away. A more detailed definition as to how Slapton Sands would be used was issued on July 7 1943. It would be required for full assault training with live firing for Force O[4] which when fully formed consisted of approximately the following:

Special Ships: 12
LST (Landing Ship, Tank) 30
Major Landing Craft 200
Minor Landing Craft 780

During the assembly and training period, these units would be based and operated from landing craft bases at Falmouth, Plymouth, Fowey, Salcombe, Dartmouth and Teignmouth, and in addition embarkation would take place from Hards at Torquay and Brixham. In addition to major exercises, small units would train and operate from Dartmouth and Salcombe.

A more detailed specification from a military point of view for combined Assault Training Area was also created.

A combined assault training area should have a frontage and depth of not less than 8,000 yards and 10,000 yards respectively. The exact dimensions of each area will be governed by the topography. The dimensions were based on the following factors:

1. a) The firefight of the Assault Division will start on the beaches and end on the consolidation of their final objective, which will normally be 8,000 to 9,000 yards inland. Thus the final phase will involve shooting on to the final objective. It is essential that the firefight should be practiced in its entirety and a depth of 10,000 yards will therefore be required.

   b) Throughout its depth the assault will be subject to interference from the flanks and firing to a flank will therefore be necessary if training is to be realistic. Assuming that the landing beaches are approximately in the centre of the sea frontage of the area a total frontage of 8,000 yards will be required[5].

2. Easy exits from the beaches

3. A convenient beach upon which large signal exercises without firing can take place.

4. Adequate quartering facilities within reasonable distance, within 30 miles, of the combined assault training area.
5. Good additional hinterland training areas suitably situated with regard to the troops' quarters.
6. Reasonable climatic conditions.

The necessary reconnaissances of the proposed South West beach areas were carried out on 3 August 1943. A combined reconnaissance of Slapton Sands, Bigbury Bay, Veryan Bay and St Austell Bay were carried out by a team comprising of:

Captain W.B Hynes RN
Lieutenant Colonel R.O. Bare USMC
Major J.I. Littlewood RA
Mr S.G. Fowler, Surveyor of Lands, Devonport, for Dartmouth Area
Mr A.C. Morgan, representing surveyor of lands Devonport for Cornwall

The ATASC Team noted that there were five potential beaches in the South Devon area[6]:

Blackpool Beach – 600 yards
Slapton Sands northern section – 800 yards
Slapton Sands southern section – 1,800 yards
Bee Sands – 600 yards
Hall Sands – 700 yards

Regarding the suitability of beaches, they noted that all were usable at all states of tide subject to weather, but that Blackpool was subject to interference from easterly weather. This area was limited to a depth of 10,000 to 13,000 yards by the Great Western Railway line from South Brent to Kingsbridge, which served all this part of South Devon.

The beach at Blackpool was mainly sand but the remainder of the beaches were formed of loose shingle with gradients up to one in six which constantly changed as a result of winds and tides. This type of beach would present a serious obstruction to the passage of both wheeled and tracked vehicles. It would be necessary to lay beach roadways on the occasion of each exercise.

They noted the unsuitability of the hinterland for vehicle deployment (both wheeled or tracked) due to the presence of sunken roads and banks, the limited number of exits from beaches, the importance of agricultural interests with valuable agricultural land affected, that the population of this area affected would exceed 1,500, and the close proximity of the main coast road running from Stoke Fleming to Torcross.

The whole beach frontage was covered by a convoy route, which was swept at frequent intervals. No special minesweeping was therefore considered necessary.

The beaches had landmines laid at various points, which would require lifting. Other beach obstacles could be left for training purposes.

They considered the whole area as not being suitable and it was not considered that all the beaches could be usefully employed for landing exercises NOT involving the firing of live ammunition and NOT involving the subsequent deployment of vehicles.

They observed that it would be possible to clear the areas behind the beaches of Slapton to a depth of 500 yards to permit the firing of rockets and smoke mortars, observing however that the great majority of the projectiles would most likely fall in water or marshland.

The recommendations of the committee were that Chesil Beach and St Austell beach were unsuitable, and that Veryan Bay was unacceptable. Captain Hymes preferred Slapton Sands, but the committee noted that unless a further reconnaissance of the Slapton area showed that use could be made of it without civilian interests needing to be dealt with quite ruthlessly, there were no suitable areas within the terms of reference of the Committee in South Devon or Cornwall.

On September 8 1943, a further reconnaissance of the Slapton area was undertaken by:

Brigadier General N.D. Cota[7] & Major Fairburn, representing ETOUSA[8].

The area initially selected comprised of two parts, defined as Area A and Area B (the latter split into two parts).

Area A comprised the bulk of the selected area, with area B comprising a smaller section of the southern part, and included the Beesands and the villages of Sherford and Chillington. General Cota was of the opinion that whilst it was agreed that these dimensions practically fulfilled the requirements prescribed by the ATASC, that if operations were to be strictly confined to the boundaries shown, training on the scale envisaged by him would be limited to an unacceptable degree, owing to the lack of sufficient vehicular exits from the beach road and the enclosed nature of the immediate hinterland. He therefore stipulated that arrangements should be made for landing, and manoeuvring rights obtained over a natural exit from the beach over the immediate hinterland, together with manoeuvring rights over all the public highways bounding the perimeter of all the areas.

He also noted that use of covering fire in areas B.1 and B.2 would be liable to cause the destruction of the villages of Torcross, Stokenham, Chillington, and Sherford, together with the 11,000–volt overhead electric cable line to the BBC station at Start Point and the 50,000–gallon reservoir at Sherford Cross with its 4–inch pipeline to Prawle. It was considered that activities in these areas must be restricted to manoeuvring rights without firing.

The possibility of restricting the limits of fire in areas so as to avoid the four villages of Blackawton, East Allington, Strete and Slapton was discussed but considered impracticable on account of their locations. It was also noted that a number of the principle residences in the area occupied commanding positions in relation to the sea approaches. These too would be likely to suffer the effects of gunfire.

On 20 October 1943 the process of examination of the possible assault training areas on the southwest coast, in west Wales, and in Scotland was completed. For the southwest coast, the Slapton Sands was selected and would involve full assault training; firing and manoeuvring throughout the area; to be requisitioned under defence regulation 51; and completely evacuated. The area was required for use by use by 1 January 1944[9].

The requirement to requisition such a large area of land was not taken lightly. It was a decision that had to be taken by the War Cabinet who met on Wednesday 3 November to discuss the issue. Amongst those present were Deputy Prime Minister Clement Attlee (Chairman), the First Lord of the Admiralty A.V. Alexander, the Minister of Agriculture and Fisheries R.S. Hudson, Lord Sherwood, Parliamentary Under-Secretary for Air, the Secretary of State for War Sir James Grigg, the Vice-Chief of the Imperial General Staff Lieut-General A.E. Nye, the Minister of Health Ernest Brown and Sir Findlater Stuart, Home Defence Executive[10].

The meeting had before them a report by the interdepartmental committee on combined training areas in which were set out the problems to be faced if the service requirements in Devon, Wales, and Scotland were to be met.

The meeting heard that the proposed new training areas were required as part of preparations for cross-channel operations, and the training they would provide was absolutely essential if that operation was to be a success. The areas finally put forward by the services authorities after the most careful reconnaissance were the only areas that provided the necessary facilities. Nevertheless, attention needed to be drawn to the ministers of the serious consequences of the proposals.

General Nye stated that the need for these areas for the success of the cross-channel offensive could not be over-stressed. Combined operations were always the most difficult of all war operations to carry out, for each of the three services was primarily designed and trained to carry out its own particular tasks and in a combined operation the need for a common doctrine and a unified control had to be enforced upon each and thoroughly understood in advance. There were broadly speaking two problems in any such operation: firstly, to get ashore and secondly to maintain oneself there. In the first our troops would be faced with first class defences: concrete emplacements with heavy guns, wire and the like which the enemy had erected on the Channel coast. Before our troops could land, sufficient fire-power must be mustered to subdue these defences and this involved bombardment by naval guns, bombing planes and heavy fire from landing craft and other sea borne or amphibious equipment manned by the army. The crucial problem was to bring down this fire on the enemy defences and then lift it at the last possible moment before our troops went in to land. The whole presented a very tricky problem of coordination and the need for the most thorough training was self-evident.

The next problem was the maintenance of the troops ashore after the first assault. This also involved training in coastal areas with suitable beaches. The Chiefs of Staff had considered very carefully whether the follow-up could be rehearsed in inland areas but had come to the conclusion that since the operational control would still at this stage be exercised from vessels at sea, the training must of necessity be in a suitable coastal zone. There was in short no possible substitute for the procedure of going through the whole process of landing and follow-up in places as closely similar as possible to those where the offensive landings would eventually be made. The areas now before the meeting had been selected from this point of view, and it could be stated with certainty that the success of the attack on the continent when it came would depend upon this decision as to whether or not these training areas should be provided.

Regarding Slapton Sands the agricultural consequences of the proposal were serious, as was clear from the facts given in the report before the meeting. The Minister for Health, Ernest Brown said that the problem of finding accommodation for the dispossessed residents would be difficult but not impossible. The estimated number of people who would require official assistance in finding new homes was 2,720, and that perhaps 1,800 would be able to make private arrangements. The problem had been discussed at a meeting of local officials presided over by the regional commissioner, and questionnaires had been prepared for issue to members of the public in the area as soon as the decision to requisition was taken. As an interim measure, temporary accommodation would be available in hostels which had been provided for homeless refugees from Plymouth, and the bulk of the displaced population would no doubt eventually be found homes in Torquay and Paignton, which had fortunately been cleared some time ago of evacuees from air-raid danger areas. Ernest Brown also acknowledged that there was a compensation gap as a result of the limits of the Compensation (Defence) Act, and that in his view the most serious problem was that of the small shopkeeper or trader removed from the area, who would lose his only livelihood. Special provision for the compensation of people in this class was clearly desirable.

Sir James Grigg commented it would be difficult to compensate people in full for loss of livelihood under the existing statutes, which provided for compensation for loss of rent but not for loss of profit. Any attempt to change this position would involve a change in the whole basis of the Compensation Acts and the better course would be to deal with problems of this kind by stretching the existing law to the limit. In the case of certain small areas from which the War Office had found it necessary to evacuate the residents, a small fund had by agreement with the Treasury been placed at the disposal of the Regional Commissioner to enable him to help hard cases, and possibly something on these lines could be done at Slapton Sands.

It was acknowledged that the important telecommunications service installations in the vicinity, and the BBC transmitters at Start Point, might well be damaged during training operations. Presumably the risk of this was appreciated and accepted by the interested departments, but the Post Office should nevertheless be given every facility for rapid repair.

It was noted that the Home Secretary was most anxious for instructions to be issued to the troops actually undergoing training that they should do everything possible to avoid damaging the many valuable and historic buildings in the area.

General Nye agreed that this was a very reasonable request, which should be met. The Minister of Agriculture and Fisheries, Mr R.S. Hudson stated that it would be helpful if the dispossessed farmers could be given some idea how long the area would be required for training.

The First Lord of the Admiralty pointed out that for security reasons it would be inadvisable to give the farmers an approximate date on which the area would cease to be required. The Secretary of State for War, Sir James Grigg suggested that the farmers should be advised to find temporary accommodation elsewhere, it being made quite clear without any definite references to time that they would be allowed to return later. This was agreed to.

The scene was set, with approval given at the highest ministerial level. The Slapton Sands area, along with its unwitting inhabitants, was to play a major part in the forthcoming invasion of mainland Europe.

## Chapter Six

# Compensation – The British Way

With the plans now confirmed that the Slapton Area was to be evacuated to provide the necessary amphibious training, the thorny question of how to recompense the displaced population had to be addressed. In 1943 the cold fact was that the country was embroiled in a major war for survival and that to win, the offensive would have to be taken to the heart of the enemy. To do this a massive cross-channel attack would be necessary to gain a foothold in mainland Europe. The financial logistics of supporting a massive war effort produced a huge burden that required delicate financial management. The Chancellor of the Exchequer and the Treasury still held the purse strings in war as it did in peacetime. The compensation issue would show the best and worst of the British governmental system.

A battle developed between the position of Treasury and between those that believed this was not a simple matter of applying the law but about fairness to those who would be dispossessed by the forthcoming evacuation. The existing mechanism to manage compensation for this type of event had to be assessed in accordance with the provisions of Section 2 of the Compensation (Defence) Act, 1939. The trouble was this act was not originally conceived to manage events of the scale of the Slapton area evacuation, which would be far larger than anything of this type that had occurred before. The area to be evacuated would comprise 19,840 acres with 2,750 people; 765 families would have to be evacuated. Altogether 180 farms, 28 shops, 11 inns, 1 hotel, 100 houses, and 450 cottages would need to be vacated for an uncertain period of time. Farmers, shopkeepers, businesses and individuals would find themselves possibly out of a job, or having to suspend businesses, or in some cases to close them down permanently.

Whilst the remit of the Compensation (Defence) Act could allow compensation to be paid for some aspects of the evacuation, there were many that it did not cover. It made no allowance for the payment of compensation to farmers for the loss or forced sale of farming stock or implements, nor did it provide for the payment of compensation to shopkeepers, innkeepers, etc for loss of trade or goodwill.

It was recognised that many farmers would need to take jobs as farm hands in which capacities they would be paid considerably less than they had been earning on their own. A survey of the area indicated that thirty-nine individual shopkeepers and innkeepers would not be compensated for loss of profit and goodwill. Additionally between fifty and seventy-five people who derived income by taking in lodgers during the summer holiday season would also receive no recompense.

The official line from the Treasury was that the state should not accept responsibility for 'hardship' occurring as a result of the war. They argued that there was no difference whatever in principle between the disposed shopkeeper whose business is lost or seriously interfered with as a result of enemy action, than that whose losses resulted from government actions as a consequence of war conditions[1].

From some officials a decidedly unsympathetic tone was forthcoming. One such unnamed official commenting on the First Lord of The Admiralty's concerns stated on 21 December 1943: 'I think the First Lord a little under-estimates the amount of the help that can be given within the existing law. Loss on the forced sale by a farmer of stock or implements can be reimbursed; (this has never in practice been necessary, for forced sales have generally shown a very large advance in process). It is true that we have no power to compensate shopkeepers or innkeepers for the loss of profits on trading, but if they are able-bodied persons, they will have no difficulty in obtaining work which will at least give them a livelihood and if they are crippled or aged, the Assistance Board can help them. Surely reluctance to go to the Assistance Board cannot be accepted as a reason for providing a substitute.'[2]

Certainly for the farmers the prospect of being evacuated did not look good. A separate official report acknowledged that, 'As far as can be ascertained there are no suitable alternative farms available in the region, hence it appears that most of these farmers will have to be put out of business, which involves the sale or slaughter of over 10,000 head of livestock excluding poultry.'[3]

To those closer to the problem a more sympathetic stance was that this could scarcely apply in the case of farmers and small shopkeepers deliberately dispossessed by the state. Here the loss of business or goodwill was not so much a hardship as a definite, and in some cases a permanent, injury. Those of this opinion included Sir Hugh Elles, the Regional Commissioner[4] of the Kingsbridge Rural District Council, the First Lord of the Admiralty A.V. Alexander[5], and the local Member of Parliament Colonel Ralph Rayner.

To cater for the compensation categories not included in the existing Act the law would need to be changed; and there was no time or real political will to do this.

The battle lines were drawn between those who considered it fair that people whose lives should be turned upside down as result of having been displaced for the greater good (particularly for the US Allies) should be compensated, and those in the Treasury who appeared to be more concerned about applying the law.

Those whose views ran counter to that of the Treasury in defence of these views rather pointedly stated: 'While every member of the community is liable to suffer from the rigours of enemy action or from the general consequences of war, the case here is that particular individuals are being selected to undergo abnormal hardship simply because the area in which they happen to live is the most convenient for the state's operations – in other words the burden borne by them is not shared by the community as a whole.'

In another government memo dated 30 November 1943 a department under-secretary also concurs with the lack of fairness: 'I do not see that it is defensible for the state to destroy property by a deliberate act, and then to refuse compensation. It is by no means the same if an enemy bomb falls on the premises and destroys them.'[6]

It was recognised that whilst a good case existed, pressure would still have to be exerted by interested ministers on the Chancellor, Sir John Anderson, and that even so the chances of success were small.

Desperately seeking a solution, a number of options were considered. In a similar case, referred to as 'the East Anglia case', the War Office had been able to arrange for what was described as 'some modification of the hardships suffered by dispossessed tradesmen, farmers, etc'.[7] Here an approach had been made to a charity, the Pilgrims Trust, who had made a charitable grant of £1,000. Whilst it was recognised that an amount of a £1,000 would be inadequate for the level of compensation required for the Slapton area evacuation, perhaps other suitable charities could be approached. The First Lord of the Admiralty A.V. Alexander highlighted the potential problems this approach. It could lead to invidious comparisons between the generosity of charitable institutions and the evident hard-heartedness of government. Additionally, it would be stipulated that any charitable source could not be disclosed. This could easily have created additional embarrassment for government, as not only would they have to concede that the dispossessed had needed to turn to charity, but also that government would not even allow the charitable source to be disclosed.

The First Lord urged that either the home Secretary or the Chancellor should be approached and that this issue was the responsibility of government and should not be left to the benevolence of war charities or other charitable organisations.

A.V. Alexander himself wrote to the Chancellor raising these strong moral arguments. Despite this the Chancellor was unmoved; the British Government were not going to pay for any additional compensation not covered by the Compensation (Defence) Act.

The formal response of the Chancellor's office once again raised the idea of seeking additional funds from a charitable source: 'The chancellor said that he had considered the First Lord's representations very carefully but had come to the conclusion that he could not act upon them without opening other doors to an entirely unacceptable extent. The chancellor therefore proposed to obtain funds from American charitable sources in order to provide increased assistance for disposed residents of the Slapton Sands area.'[8]

Alexander's response to this was, if this was all that could be hoped for he would have no objection. He had tried, but could do no more.

Whilst the Government was determined to uphold the principle that the state should not accept responsibility for hardship, officials were also noting the negative effect this could have on public opinion. A government memo dated 14 December 1943 stated: 'Nevertheless a case of wholesale requisition seems to be one to demand special treatment. Naturally I think it appeals to ones feeling of sympathy more poignantly. Apart from this it is more liable to come to the notice of general public and if the principles of the Act are to be upheld, exceptional steps to mitigate cases of hardship are politically desirable.' Even during wartime, the realities of politics are never far from the minds of politicians and Government Officials.

The local MP meanwhile had also independently been busy following the charitable route. Colonel Ralph Rayner had been the Member of Parliament for the Totnes constituency since 1935. A career soldier, he had served in the First World War and subsequently served as ADC to the Governor General of Canada before entering politics in 1935[9]. He was now serving once again in the Army as a Colonel and Chief Signal Officer at Lisburn in Northern Ireland. Rayner had visited 10 Downing Street on 29 January 1944 and raised the issue with the Parliamentary Private Secretary to Winston Churchill, Brigadier Harvie-Watt MP. Following the meeting, Rayner wrote to Harvie-Watt on 1 February 1944:

My Dear Harvie-Watt,

This is the richest and most important area in Great Britain ever to be taken over on complete evacuation of its inhabitants. Nine villages and over two hundred farmers have been affected. Nearly all concerned have shown a fine spirit of cooperation but the hardships are many and my constituency trays are now full of appeals and of details of hard cases which can in no way be covered by the 1939 Act. These consist mainly of losses under the following heads:

1. Owner farmers are thrown out of their farms just when many of them for the first time for years are making good money. They lose the opportunity moreover should they so desire of selling their farms at a high price on a rising market. In addition to loss of livelihood they have also lost on forced sales of stock and produce.
2. Tenant farmers equally lose livelihood and on forced sales.
3. Hotel keepers, of which there are many, who have been keeping their businesses going on accommodation of elderly people, lose their livelihoods as it is almost impossible nowadays to open up elsewhere. Many of them lose on removal. For example, one retired officer had just fitted his whole hotel with linoleum which when torn out was

worth little. Normally all these sorts of things would have been taken over by the incoming tenant on valuation.

4.  Small traders (dozens of butchers, bakers, general stores, etc) lose both livelihood and on forced sales and it is quite impossible to open up elsewhere under present restrictions.

The 1939 act covers none of the above losses and quite obviously nothing can or will be done to amend that Act to embrace loss of profit or goodwill. Such amendment would lead to all kinds of retrospective complications and take the government into very deep waters. Meanwhile many of those turned out lose badly for I could give you plenty of definite cases under all the above heads.

I attach copy of a broadcast made by me over the Columbia network last Thursday January 27th. This was of course approved by the MOI.

I wish now to liaise with certain unofficial American organisations with a view to securing some funds for hard cases among evacuees in areas leased to the American Forces. This I suggest will have the following advantages:

1.  Allow fair cover for hard cases under the 1939 act.
2.  Encourage Americans to take an interest in the areas loaned to them and form another of those ties we are all trying to forge.

I have talked this matter over with Mr Phillip Reed who made several helpful suggestions and also with various other responsible Americans all of whom are in favour.

Sir John Daw (Chairman) and Devon County Council are fully with me and would take responsibility for any funds collected and allotted to Devon.

I would like to know whether the PM would have any objection to this private project and will be most grateful if you would discuss the matter with J.M. Martin and whoever else you feel should be consulted. All I am asking for is a note saying No.10 has no objection.

Sincerely,
Ralph Rayner

The radio broadcast Rayner had made on the American Columbia Network (the Columbia Broadcasting Service, better known today as CBS) had stirred up a bit of a hornets' nest within government. The broadcast had apparently been made with full permission from the Ministry of Information but, when reviewed from the perspective of No.10 it had been noted as containing 'less felicitous' phrases, for example: 'the ungenerous Act of 1939'. And, no doubt to help American listeners better understand the situation, Colonel Rayner had made a comparison to the affect of an assault training area being created in California for use by British Forces.

As it happened, unknown to Ralph Rayner, both the Admiralty and the Treasury were already pursuing the American charitable route for funds.

Concerns in government were raised, as the broadcast could prove embarrassing to the British Government, as representations had already been made to the US Ambassador John Winant. It was feared that if Colonel Rayner's broadcast, which was seen from a British Government perspective as attempting to 'raise the wind in America' came to his attention, this might damage the cause.[10]

As a result it was considered that it would be best if Colonel Rayner did not deal unofficially with the Americans. As a result Rayner was 'warned off' in a very polite manner by No.10 in relation to his unofficial approaches.

10 Downing St, SW1
February 10, 1944.

Dear Ralph,

I have made enquiries regarding the hardship amongst people evacuated in the American Assault area about which you wrote to me on February 1.

The Prime Minister has been personally consulted, but we have discussed the matter here. As you probably know, the Admiralty are the department responsible for taking the action to requisition and I understand that at the moment they and the Treasury are in touch with the Americans for the very purposes which you have in mind. Our feeling is that it might be wiser not to open up more than one channel of communication with the Americans and that it would therefore be better for you to await the result of the discussions which are now taking place. I hope that this will be found satisfactory to you and your constituents.

Yours ever,
Harvie-Watt

Meanwhile the American route was being pursued by approaching the American Red Cross. Unofficially sounding out the idea however had caused some major concerns with this avenue of approach. There appeared to be no doubt that the American Red Cross would make a very great play with publicity if they were to contribute funds to this charitable cause. There would be photographs and interviews. There would be press headlines to show how the great generous American public have come to the rescue of the poor British. From a British perspective this was viewed as being extremely injurious to British prestige whilst appearing extremely favourable to American prestige. If the American Red Cross decided to publicise any donation there would be nothing the government could do about this. The Foreign Office were strongly against any publicity and stated that they would 'be very much against any publicity about the proposed American gesture either here or in the USA.[11]

With the prospect of this unpalatable publicity, the option to approach the American Red Cross had become much less appealing than originally hoped.

The ball had now been batted back to the British Government to once more look to paying compensation to their citizens themselves.

In desperation, a proposal was put forward to allow covert direction of government funding via a charitable cause. One official had recalled that during the Invergordon Mutiny of 1931, in which sailors of the home fleet had mutinied protesting about a cut in pay, the government had found a way out of the difficult situation they had got themselves into by covertly subsidising the Royal Naval Benevolent Trust who presumably then passed on donations to those sailors in need.

Another idea in a similar vein was raised where direct assistance from the Exchequer in the form of disguised payments could be made by some local relief fund which could be reimbursed in private behind the scenes. The originator of this idea was of the opinion that this course of action would enable the Treasury faithfully to say that no payments had been made from the Exchequer to individuals who have been dispossessed of their property or business outside the ordinary requisition code. It appears that these covert ideas were not pursued in any way.[12]

In the real world however, the compensation issue or rather the lack of it was starting to become a growing political issue. On 13 November the Rural District Council of Kingsbridge wrote a formal letter to the Regional Commission and all the local MPs. This letter detailed a formal resolution passed by the council on 19 November 1943 and stated:

At a special meeting of members of this council held on Wednesday last the 19th instant the following resolution was passed namely:

'The Kingsbridge Rural District Council desire to put on record their wish to co-operate loyally in every way with the evacuation scheme but they urge emphatically that if the minimum of hardship is to be caused and grave injustice avoided full compensation for loss of business and goodwill and other losses not covered by the 1939 Act must be provided.

The council will be grateful if you would be good enough to let me know that you support the resolution.'[13]

One of the local MPs was the ex-Minister for War, Leslie Hore-Belisha. No longer in a position of power, but still a high profile politician, Hore-Belisha, wrote to A.V. Alexander to enquire as to what the position was regarding this. Alexander replied to Hore-Belisha on the 12 December 1943 stating:

I am writing in reply to your letter of November 25th to me and your letter of November 16th to Morrison, copy of a resolution passed by the Kingsbridge Rural District Council. As you are aware this area has been selected as a result of strategic planning on a high level and I should explain that the Admiralty is merely the agent in carrying out the decision to requisition. I can assure you that my lands branch are doing and will continue to do our best for the people who are affected by this disturbance but as I am sure you appreciate we are limited in what we can do by an act of parliament.

A non-committal answer, but the pressure to sort out the compensation issue was growing.

The story was also starting to be picked up in the newspapers. *The Daily Express* on 16 December 1943 ran a short piece stating:

Southwest England farmers, whose land has been taken over as an American battle school, yesterday saw flocks of sheep auctioned at rock-bottom prices. Rams, which cost £21 each, were sold for £4 15s. Thousands of sheep went for £1 or £2 less than they cost last autumn and spring. One farmer said: 'The sale is out of season for breeding sheep. It is a pity the authorities didn't tell us earlier we would have to leave, then we could have sold in the autumn. We are relying on the government to give us the difference between the sale price and proper value'.

A letter to *The Times* on the 14 December 1943 raised this issue in more detail:

Evacuation Claims

To the editor of *The Times*

Sir, As one not directly affected by the evacuation in the Southwest, but a near neighbour of the sufferers, may I express the general dissatisfaction which we feel at Mr Alexander's answer given in parliament on December 8? It has not been possible, he says, to give any guarantee against pecuniary loss, because 'compensation has to be paid in accordance with the provisions of the Compensation (Defence) Act 1939' and he can only promise that all claims will be subject to that limitation. If they cannot be met under existing legislation, let the law be altered. What else are our lawyer's legislators for, but to see that justice is done? As taxpayers and electors we have a right to demand on behalf of our neighbours that legislative difficulties should not be allowed as an excuse for adding avoidable pecuniary loss to the unavoidable personal sacrifices which are being so patiently and patriotically accepted. For that patient acceptance and for the admirable and sympathetic efficiency of the helpers whom the government have sent down, we have nothing but praise and admiration. But unless full compensation is paid much of the good work done by these helpers will be frustrated and a rankling sense of legitimate grievance will remain,

Frank Fletcher

The issue had in fact been raised in Parliament by Daniel Frankel, the Member of Parliament for Stepney Mile End on 8 December 1943. Mr Frankel had asked as to what arrangements had been made in relation to compensation for hardships to the inhabitants of the area resulting from the evacuation; had any special organisation been set-up to deal with the problem; what arrangements, if any, had been made to preserve monuments and buildings of architectural or other value and properties of peculiar agricultural or horticultural value; and were the Americans aware of this?

A.V. Alexander, responded, on behalf of the Government: *Mr. Frankel* asked the First Lord of the Admiralty the arrangements which have been made to meet the hardships of the inhabitants of a certain part in the South-Western area who have been evacuated to make room for troops; and particularly what provision was made for transportation to alternative accommodation; what guarantee was given against pecuniary loss through the compulsory disposal of property, stock and other effects; and what guarantees have been given for the restoration to these people of their homes when the time arrives, together with the assistance to enable them to re-establish themselves when the restoration takes place?

*Mr. Alexander:* Every endeavour is being made to meet the hardships of the people evacuated from this area. Arrangements have been made to obtain living accommodation for those who are unable to obtain alternative accommodation themselves. Immediate monetary advances are being made in respect of expenses incurred in removal, and free storage accommodation is being provided for property which they cannot take with them. An endeavour is being made to find work for those who have no other employment to which they can transfer. A car pool is available to transport people to alternative accommodation in the immediate vicinity or to the nearest railway station in the case of people moving to a distance, and a motor transport pool with the necessary labour has been organised for removing their belongings. Assistance is also being provided for packing and so on, for those unable to do the work themselves.

Compensation has to be paid in accordance with the provisions of the Compensation (Defence) Act 1939, and consequently it has not been possible to give any guarantee against pecuniary loss. All claims, however, are being dealt with as generously as possible under the Act. It is anticipated that the provision of storage accommodation for furniture and other effects and the arrangements which have been made for maintaining livestock on other farms outside the area will mean that very few people will have to dispose of their property, stock and other effects. People affected have been told that the area will be released from requisition as soon as Service requirements permit and that just as every assistance is being given to them in evacuating the area, so will all possible aid be given in re-establishing them later.

*Mr. Frankel*: Is any special organisation being set up to deal with representations in respect of particular cases of hardship?

*Mr. Alexander:* All that has been communicated to the people on the spot.

*Mr. Godfrey Nicholson*: What arrangements, if any, have been made to preserve monuments and buildings of architectural or other value and properties of peculiar agricultural or horticultural value?

*Mr. Alexander*: The Chiefs of Staff concerned are constantly in touch with each other, and are doing their best to secure the objectives my Hon. Friend has in mind.

*Mr. Nicholson*: Is my Right Hon. Friend sure that the Chiefs of Staff concerned have an appreciation of these aspects of the matter?

*Mr. Alexander*: I find that the Chiefs of Staff, who are representatives of the American nation, are as keen upon those things as we are ourselves.[14]

This gap in the method of compensation had been admitted in Parliament. The local Council had made a collective stand by forcefully stating the case against what they considered to be a grave injustice and the story had been seen in the newspapers.

Something had to be done. In a memo dated 16 December 1943 the Chief Surveyor of Lands noted the concern within the establishment itself:

'There is considerable agitation on this matter, including representations by Sir Hugh Elles, the Regional Commissioner, to the Ministry of Home Security. The A.S. (C.L.) is putting up a personnel letter for the 1st Lord to send to the Chancellor in an attempt to obtain a small fund from which payments could be made in cases were compensation under the Act alone cause exceptional distress.'

The fact still remained that the evacuation was taking place in mid-winter at very short notice in a county which was already heavily populated with the result that alternative accommodation both for man and beast was at a premium.

There were people in humble circumstances, for example old-age pensioners, people who had lived in a village most of their lives and had put the whole of their savings into their houses. Compensation for many would make the difference between living in some degree of comfort and amenity and living in poverty. It was acknowledged that officials were untiring in their efforts and were ready to do everything to help people. It was felt that many people were reluctant to apply for assistance through pride and perhaps feeling that it was simply a form of charity rather than a genuine compensation for state driven disturbance. On a wider theme, there was no doubt that every member of the community was liable to suffer from the general consequences of the war. But surely the particular individuals suffering due to this enforced evacuation were being selected to undergo abnormal hardship simply because of the area in which they happened to live? In other words, they were being asked to bear a burden which was not shared by the community as a whole.

There was also a psychological factor to be taken into account that the evacuation was for the benefit of American troops. It was acknowledged that the inhabitants had taken this matter in a fine spirit with practically no grumbling.

Whilst this story may appear to be about fairness versus intransigent officialdom, it should be seen in the context of the time. The country, and one can argue civilisation itself, was in the midst of a war for survival.

What can be seen is that the rights of those less fortunate were still being stood up for, despite the stance of the Treasury, who one could argue were only doing their job. If the same story had being occurring in Nazi Germany or any of the countries occupied by Nazis, no doubt the story would have been very different. Compensation would not have been the major concern.

*Chapter Seven*

# Compensation – The Americans to the Rescue

The idea of a small fund was still being worked on at the end of 1943. Despite the various attempts to fill the compensation gap, none had so far been successful. The Treasury were not going to be moved on the point of principle. The American Red Cross solution had been rejected due to the perceived negative public relations impact it would have had on the nation and particularly the Government. The idea to provide governmental 'back-door' funding had also not been followed up. It would be the generosity of the Americans that would finally provide a solution.

Conversations with the American Ambassador John Winant had produced a favourable response. He considered that a contribution could possibly be made from US Army funds. He had passed the issue to one of his staff, US Army Colonel William Ganoe.

After an initial discussion, Colonel Ganoe identified two possible sources of army funding. To proceed further he required more detail of how and what the fund might be used for, and an indication of the possible amounts involved. A problem from the British perspective was that the colonel seemed to have a sum of only £2,000 in mind. It seems the he had not been briefed in any degree of detail, as he also seemed to be under the impression that the level of compensation currently available had been provided under Elizabethan Poor Laws rather than more recent acts of parliament. The relevant level of detail was to be supplied and a meeting with Colonel Ganoe and the Admiralty was arranged to help clear things up and also to attempt to increase the level of funding.

British government officials struggled to meet the colonel's request for an estimate of the sum required to deal with hardship cases amongst the Slapton evacuees (with some details to explain its basis). The difficulty in meeting this request was that whilst some examples of hardship claims had been recorded, due to the absence of a mechanism to formally deal with these claims, no comprehensive list existed of people who might claim under the hardship category. Using only the specimen cases, no firm estimate could be made of realistic sums. Only a draft statement and figure could be provided to the Americans.

Based on the information available, the size of the fund required was estimated to be approximately £10,000. The British officials however, were reticent in putting this figure before Colonel Ganoe as this was somewhat more than he was expecting.

The Treasury were under pressure to get the necessary information to the colonel. One official noted in relation to a request for further information:

'Colonel Ganoe is on my tail and I gather the Ambassador is on his, so that I should appreciate a very early reply for this reason if no other. The other reason is that some of the evacuees have lost their sources of income for over a month now.'[1]

This provides a somewhat interesting insight into his priorities.

By 25 January 1944, whilst no comprehensive figures were available, the level of hardship incurred that could not be catered for under the existing legislation, was estimated at:

*Householders*

| | |
|---|---|
| Farmer and Smallholders | 184 |
| Lodging and Boarding Houskeepers | 50 |
| Shopkeepers | 25 |
| Innkeepers | 11 |
| Cottagers | 500 |
| Total | 770 |

*Farmers and Smallholders* (particulars not available)

| | |
|---|---|
| Lodging and boarding house keepers | 25 |
| Shopkeepers | 25 |
| Innkeepers | 11 |
| Cottagers etc. | 200 |
| Total | 261 |

The level of hardship was acknowledged to vary in each case but a representative allowance was calculated as:

25 Lodging and boarding house keepers @ £3 a week:   £75 a week
25 Shopkeepers @ £3 a week                           £75 a week
11 Innkeepers @ £3 a week                            £33 a week
200 Cottagers for difference of rent @ 5/- a week    £50 a week
Total:                                               £233 a week

An allowance for farmers and smallholders of whose cases no details were yet available was included and estimated at £17 per week, which brought the weekly total for all cases to an estimated £250 per week.[2]

The total length of time this would be needed was unknown but assumed to be six months for the actual evacuation plus three months for re-settlement. Using these estimated figures, a figure of £10,000 pounds was estimated as being required.

For many, the meaning of the word 'hardship' is somewhat subjective. It must be borne in mind that this occurred during a time before the existence of the welfare state. There are documents existing in the National Archive at Kew in London that describe some cases and perhaps give a more objective understanding of what 'hardship' actually meant for some of the individuals suffering as a result of the forced evacuation. Three examples of the effect on lodging and boarding housekeepers were cited:

Mrs Maunder, Highcliff House, Strete. Guest house. (Widow. Boy of 3. Mother OAP. Income £40, now living on capital)

Miss E. Oldfield, Slapton. (Age 60, and physically incapable of taking up new work)

The Misses Woods, Fairfield, Chillington. (Sole livelihood, letting rooms and running market garden, both gone)

An example of a hotelkeeper and innkeeper were also cited:

Mrs. Lavers, Queens Arms Hotel, Slapton. (Widow. Age 45–50. Son at secondary school. In 18 months has lost husband, daughter, business and home)

Mr. Jones, Fortescue Arms, East Allington (Has recently taken the license, and has done much and spent a lot of money in bringing the inn up to a fine standard)

For the shopkeepers three examples were cited:

Mr. Foale, The Stores, Blackawton. (150 registered customers. Has no prospect of getting new business. Estimates loss £5 a week)

C.L.R. Wills, Ivy View Strete. (Boot repairer. He is now in Loddiswell, and says that his business is 'clean gone')

Mr. J.H. Pike, Lily side, Torcross. (Fishermans Supply store, which was sole means of support)

For the farmers and small-holder two cases were detailed:

Lynn, Home Farm, Sherford. (Owner, who had sunk all his capital in it and was making a comfortable living. No capital to buy a new one. Has gone to a flat in Kingsbridge and is looking for a job)

Mr. and Mrs. Oldrieve, Sheperds Cottage, Blackawton. (Small-holders. Old age pensioners. Cannot find any work. No supplementary pension)

The question had been raised by the Americans regarding British unemployment payments. The position regarding this was explained under the current wartime situation that this was available to those who could show that they would normally be in employment and were capable of, and available for work.

This was as defined under Section 36 of the Unemployment Assistance Act 1934. During wartime a new regulation had been made under the provisions of the Emergency Powers (Defence) Act 1939 to widen the criteria as to how unemployment assistance could be granted. It also could now be granted to a person of at least 16 years who was in distress owing to circumstances caused by the war, either because they had been evacuated under Government arrangements, or they or some person on whom they were normally dependent had lost their employment or could not follow their normal occupation or had lost their normal means of livelihood. The amount granted by the Unemployment Assistance Board was dependent on the amount needed by the applicant, measured on a scale laid down by regulations. A married couple without other resources were regarded as needing 31/- a week (exclusive of rent), with other appropriate rates for other types of applicants and for dependants.

It was pointed out that this was not a form of compensation; it was merely designed to prevent and alleviate distress.

With the further details now with the American benefactors, the British now waited. On 14 February 1944, the Treasury noted, 'I do not know anything more that can be done to help the Americans take the plunge!'[3]

On 3 March 1944 Colonel Ganoe indicated that he was practically in a position to promise some money and a figure of £3,000 was quoted.

On the 16 March 1944 a spanner appeared to have been thrown into the works. A meeting took place with Brigadier General Edward C. Betts,[4] the American Judge Advocate, European Theatre of Operations. In this meeting the US Authorities had apparently given instructions that the grant of funds should not be proceeded with. The reason given was that the Americans themselves had to make evacuations in the United States for training purposes on a similar scale to those made here, but they did not propose to provide any assistance to the dispossessed such as was proposed in the Slapton evacuation area. Consequently they did not see how grants could be made towards the relief of people in this country, which would be refused for their own nationals. Whilst still appreciative of the difficulties being experienced by those involved in the Slapton evacuation area and anxious to help, they admitted that they were now very gloomy of the outcome.[5]

However, on 20 March Colonel Ganoe reported that the situation had been reversed and that 'someone was on his way from the United States with a scheme and some money in his pocket'. This someone was Major Edwin Rives[6]. Major Rives was a trained lawyer who had also been a judge prior to the war and was now working for the US Army Judge Advocate General's Department. He had been entrusted with setting up the scheme to assist the Slapton Evacuees, which the British couldn't or wouldn't help. Major Rives got to work quickly. He met with the Regional Commissioner Sir Hugh Elles, visited the Lands Branch at Bath, and visited the Regional Commissioner's Office in Bristol. As a result, on 11 April 1944 he reported to the Treasury that he felt confident he would be able to obtain a grant of £6,000, which he considered to be the actual amount required as a result of his local enquiries.

On 28 April 1944, Sir John Anderson wrote to John Winant stating that the American Army Authorities had made a grant of £6,000 to the Regional Commissioner for the assistance of the Slapton Evacuees and emphasised that this was a generous gesture which would bring relief to very many cases of genuine hardship and distress. He acknowledged that he was most grateful for all that had been done to set this scheme up.

Replying, Ambassador Winant responded that he was very glad to hear what had been done and hoped it would bring relief to many cases of hardship and distress.

The Committee was set up and included the following members:

Chairman.   Sir John Daw, Chairman, Devon County council
Members.    Major E.E. Rives, United States Army
            Mr. K.G. Harper, Regional Commissioner's Office
            Mr. W.G.E. Quick, Devon War Agricultural Executive
            Committee.
            Mr. R.E. Tuckett, Admiralty Lands Branch
            Mr. E.G. Gowan, Assistance board (by turns)
            Mr.L. Hampton
            Mr.R.W.Prowse, Chairman Kingsbridge RDC

The Assistance Board desired to act in an advisory capacity only. The Committee sat for fifteen days between 1 and 24 May. Eight sittings were held at Kingsbridge, four at Totnes, two at Torquay, and one at Dartmouth. Two different letters were sent out to invite people to come forward with hardship claims. The Regional Commissioner, Sir Hugh Elles had sent a letter to 209 persons whose names appeared on a 'hardship list' previously prepared from various sources available in the Regional Commissioner's office. Each of these persons was invited to appear at a named date, time and place, or to state a case in writing. Another letter was sent to all other residents in the area on a wider basis. All the recipients of this letter were invited to apply in writing and make an application if they considered themselves to be in actual distress or have suffered a serious lowering of their standard of living as a result of being evacuated. These people were invited to make a written claim.

The initial letter from Sir Hugh Elles to the specially selected 209 individuals, whilst no doubt well meaning, was a lengthy and somewhat confusing text running to nearly 700 words. It failed to succinctly deliver the message, with the simple message about eligibility to make a claims somewhat masked by over-emphasising the facts about having not been able to claim previously and featuring a somewhat rambling introduction.

The second version of the letter, sent out more widely, signed by a Principal officer of the Regional Commissioner's Office was, whilst much shorter, not much better.

As a result of these confusing letters, during the course of proceedings it became evident that the intention of these two letters had been misconstrued by those that had received them and that many people were holding back, presumably either because they didn't understand the letters or, due to the lack of clarity, assumed that they would not be eligible. The Committee therefore prepared a third letter which was sent (with some small exceptions) to all who had not already applied and who were not in receipt of a supplementary pension or PRD (Poor Relief of Distress) grant. The response to this letter was widespread and immediate.

As a result of claims received, the Committee considered 319 cases and recommended 193 awards, the list of recommendations being entrusted to Major Rives and Mr Harper of the Regional Commissioner's Office. The amount recommended for disbursement as a result of these claims was £4,740.

On the advice of the Assistance board, no immediate awards were made to persons in receipt of supplementary pension or a PRD grant, since such awards might affect the amount they may be receiving through these existing channels. As a result of this type of claim, the Committee therefore decided, with the concurrence of the Assistance Board, to recommend a grant of £10 each to 101 persons in these categories, payment to be deferred until return to the area. An additional £1,010 was earmarked for this purpose.

As a result of the claims approved, a balance of £250 remained from the original £6,000 grant. With the agreement of Major Rives, this balance was retained for use to cater for further cases of hardship that might come to light upon return to the area. With the help of the American allies, the gap in compensation had been closed. In all, 289 people received compensation by applying under the auspices of this fund. The claim amounts varied with a single maximum claim of £75 to the lowest amount of £5, claimed by six individuals, with varying amounts in between. To the 289 claimants, with even the lowest claim representing nearly an average week's wages in 1943, this must have meant a substantial amount. Whilst many fair-minded British leaders and officials had argued against the 'principled' stand of the Treasury, in the end it was the Americans who had bridged the compensation gap and come to the rescue of those dispossessed evacuees.

*Chapter Eight*

# Evacuation

The government instructions for those responsible for putting the evacuation in place started simply by stating 'the task', which was defined to be: 'The area was to be requisitioned as an assault training area in which live ammunition was to be used and must therefore be cleared of all inhabitants their stock and possessions by December 20th 1943.'[1]

Rumours and a guarded official confirmation of the evacuation appeared in early November. *The Western Morning News* on 8 November 1943 in the Late News section reported:

S.W. VILLAGES MAY BE EVACUATED
Three thousand inhabitants in half a dozen scattered hamlets and villages in one of the most beautiful parts of South-West England are wondering whether they will spend Christmas in their present homes. It is rumoured that there may be a wholesale evacuation of the population so that the area can be used by the American Army for training. They are all agricultural communities, with the exception of two coastal villages, which in peacetime catered for holiday-makers. It is also rumoured that Mr. Hudson, Minister for Agriculture, wanted to retain the area for agriculture, but that War Office requirements prevailed. Officially the Rural District Council who share the responsibility of shifting nearly a third of their population if the evacuation becomes fact, are still in the dark about the arrangements. The Chairman told a reporter last night that no official intimation had yet been received from the Ministry of Health about future plans. The vice-Chairman said: 'At present there are only rumours, but I have every reason to believe something definite will be announced next week. I do not know at what stage the hush-hush policy will be abandoned, but up to now everyone has been kept in the dark.'

Official public notification of the evacuation was performed using posters displayed around the area advertising public meetings to be held at East Allington Church at 11 am and Stokenham Church at 2.30 pm on Friday 12 November and at Blackawton Church at 11am and Stokenham Church at 2.30 pm on Saturday 13 November.

For some people, the first sight of these posters came when they visited the local shops in the villages. Many met the news with disbelief.

For the Bowles family living in Slapton, the first knowledge came after a visit to the local shop. On hearing the news from her daughter Margaret, her first reaction was of disbelief: 'don't talk up such rubbish', the idea just seemed an impossible one. How could the farmers possibly move all the cattle and everything else? [2]

The meeting took place at the appointed times and were well attended. *The Western Morning News* described the atmospheric scene at one of the Friday meetings:

> *It might have been a Sunday as the inhabitants filed into the tiny church of a South-West village yesterday. As the whisper of movement and conversation died down, the vicar rose, and the shuffling broke out again as the congregation knelt. Voices were joined in the Lord's Prayer. The vicar offered another…that the Holy Spirit should in all things rule their hearts… seats were resumed. But it was one of the strangest gatherings held in the ancient church.*

The Lord Lieutenent, Earl Fortescue, went on to address the crowd, 'To uproot you from your homes, in many cases homes of many generations is a blow to you. It is to me and everyone else, and you have our deepest sympathy.' He reminded those present that it was not the only area in the British Isles being taken over for training purposes and added, 'Do not let us forget that the Germans have taken over a great many other countries. We, I feel sure, realise that their treatment is not as mild as yours will be here.'

He explained that the matter had been taken up by the War Cabinet who had made the decision that this area was needed. He then went on to assure those present that everyone in all government departments and ministries would do their best to make sure the necessary moves as far as possible would be to areas where they had friends and performed as easily as possible. The expense of doing so would be borne by the government.

By way of further reassurance he pointed out that 'you are to be moved by departments of your own kith and kin, not by the merciless enemy' and, perhaps slightly less reassuringly, he emphasised that the Americans had made assurances that no more damage would be done to property than necessary.

He stressed that the object was to give the American Allies an opportunity of training under battle conditions, so that they can be trained to the fullest pitch of efficiency and finished by stating 'Please realise that you are doing a real service to our cause and that of the Allied Nations, as well as to yourselves, by giving up your country to them for this purpose.'

An unnamed American officer present at the meeting further stated that 'Battle inoculation' would save many lives and he knew that whatever the hardships caused by the move they would be offset by the lives of American and British soldiers that would be saved when the time came, for the lessons they were going to learn during the assault training.

To the disbelieving and shocked residents, the dreadful truth was revealed that they were required to evacuate the area and their homes to enable American troops to train for the forthcoming invasion of Europe. It is perhaps a genuine mark of the character of the population of the South Hams at that time that they would meet this news with stoicism and courage. Both those being evacuated and those that would assist working together to do what they could for the greater good. *The Western Morning News* correspondent present at one of the meetings noted that 'many are putting on a brave face, but one farmer summed up the general feeling with the simple comment: 'It is a heartbreaking thing'.

Some dissenting views were raised however. Mr H. Corson of the local Red Cross Agricultural Committee, called the evacuation a 'Despotic Order' and whilst recognising the rationale and the need to train the American troops, railed against the manner in which it had been done calling it 'most un-British'.[3]

From a purely administrative perspective, despite the short notice available, the mechanics of evacuating 750 families from the area had been organised in great detail.

The area would involve two local authorities, Kingsbridge Rural District Council and Totnes Rural District Council. Within the area of Kingsbridge RDC, the parishes of Blackawton, East Allington, Slapton, Strete, Stoke Fleming, Buckland-tout-Saints, Sherford, Stokenham and Woodleigh would be affected wholly or partially. The area of Totnes RDC included only a small part of the parish of Halwell.

To cater for the mass of enquiries that could be expected and to provide help and information for those requiring to be evacuated two information centres would be set-up at the Victory Hall Stokenham, serving the parishes of Stokenham, Slapton, Buckland-tout-Saints, Sherford and at Blackawton, East Allington, Woodleigh, Halwell, Stoke Fleming and Strete.

These would be staffed by the WVS (with assistants and clerical help as required), Admiralty Lands Officers, and representatives of: The Ministries of Food, Health, and Labour, the War Agricultural Executive Committee, The Assistance Board and Kingsbridge RDC.

It was planned that some staff would be permanently based at the centres with others only visiting them at frequent intervals. The visiting staff were required to keep the WVS officer in charge informed as to how and where they could be consulted in their absence.

The act of requisitioning itself would be carried out by the Admiralty Land Agent. The main administrative office for the evacuation authorities was located outside the evacuated area in the village of Dittisham on the River Dart at the Dittisham Court Hotel. Here representatives of the Regional Commissioner's office who would be responsible for the coordination of arrangements, along with other representatives of the various ministries and departments involved. All public contact would be managed at the information centres. The departmental representatives posted to information centres would be responsible for dealing with all questions relating to their own departments but could refer matters they could not deal with themselves to superiors at the main office at the Dittisham Court hotel.

Enquiry forms were sent out to all householders with a notice of requisition. The forms required householders to fill in details of those living at the address, their occupations, employers, details of lodgers, number of children attending school and where they attended. They were asked if they were able to find new accommodation for their family or if they required accommodation and if they required transport for furniture, how many furnished rooms they had and at what date they would be ready to move.

The forms were to be collected four days later by representatives of the WVS. The ladies of the WVS were asked to give all possible assistance in the completion of the forms and to satisfy themselves that those with personal problems and special circumstances (e.g. difficult families requiring special treatment) were fully detailed. These forms were then to be brought to the information centre for the parish concerned, where the information would be collated in a card index which would be maintained to keep an up to date record of every householder.

For those that required accommodation it was decided that those evacuated would be treated in exactly the same way as those rendered homeless by an air raid. Everybody would be encouraged to find accommodation for themselves, and experience elsewhere had shown that a large proportion would do so. Where this was not possible compulsory billeting would be required. No doubt to discourage those that thought this might result in being re-homed to an empty property it was to be made clear that this would normally take the form of billeting in occupied houses. It was most unlikely that empty houses would be made available. Special accommodation arrangements would be made as required for invalids, expectant mothers, old people, any difficult cases, or those deemed as unbilletable for any reason.

Where accommodation was provided in an occupied house outside the area, whether by private arrangement or by compulsory billeting, the occupier of the house would be entitled to a billeting allowance at the rate of 5/- a week for adults and 3/- for each child under the age of 14.

A certificate would be issued to those making their own arrangements to enable the billeting allowance to be claimed. The responsibility for billeting would be allocated to the Ministry of Health.

Owners of vehicles of any kind were encouraged to provide transport for the removal from the area of their family's furniture and effects or those of their neighbours. A special dispensation would be issued to the owners of unlicensed vehicles allowing them to use them for transport related to the evacuation. Applications for essential petrol could be made to the officer in charge of the information centre who would have the power to issue limited quantities on their own responsibility and larger amounts with the sanction of the local officer of the regional petroleum office or the regional transport commissioner.

Car pools would be established at the information centres to bring people from outlying villages to the centre, to take people to arrange housing and storage accommodation outside the area, or to a railway station or bus stop from which such journeys could be made.

Generous use of the car pool was encouraged, to avoid delay or hardship, but at the same time encouraging full use to be made of public transport, bus or rail especially, for longer journeys.

If householders were unable to make their own arrangements for the removal of their furniture, they could arrange with a furniture remover or other carrier. It was acknowledged that after an initial period all transport was likely to be controlled and would then only be obtainable through the information centres. After this period, all applications would need to give full details of the time and place at which the transport was required, the load (e.g. contents of a four-roomed cottage) and the destination. Transport would then be provided according to a planned programme designed to secure speed and economy.

The reasonable cost of all necessary journeys would be paid by the admiralty.

For those that could not accommodate all their belongings in a new residence, storage would be arranged.

The War Agricultural Committee would deal with farmers. It was acknowledged that the farming community would have particular problems relating to the completion of threshing and the disposal of livestock and these would need to be dealt with by qualified personnel at information centres.

Farm Workers and others who performed work connected with farming would also be advised to consult the War Agricultural Executive Committee who would arrange to find them work, vacant cottages, or accommodation in billets. If they did not find new posts on their own they were to notify the War Agricultural Committee who would help find them work.

Shopkeepers would be visited to make arrangements for the removal or disposal of stock. Special arrangements might be needed in cases where a village shopkeeper proposed to move in advance of the bulk of the population and in the case of a food-shop the food executive officer of Kingsbridge Rural District was to be immediately informed of each intention.

Compensation would be paid by the Admiralty in accordance with the provisions of the Compensation (Defence) Act 1939. Periodical payments in nature of rent would be made for land and buildings.

A lump sum would be paid for farm crops and garden produce on the lines of what would normally be payable by an incoming tenant in respect of growing crops, cultivations, etc., as well as expenses reasonably incurred. This would become the property of the Admiralty, but no obstacles were to be put in the way of their removal.

A lump sum would also be paid for the cost of removal of furniture, car, farm stock and implements, auction expenses, valuer's fees and loss of wages due to time spent looking for work or accommodation. Where furniture etc. had to be put into store, the reasonable cost of storage would also be reimbursed.

Where compensation was liable, Admiralty lands officers would make immediate cash payment of up to £20 in settlement of small claims, and payments on account for larger ones by cheque within three days.

Compensation was not payable for goodwill or loss of profits, but the Ministry of Food and the Board of Trade would do whatever possible to reinstate traders in business elsewhere, and the War Agricultural Executive Committee would be responsible for finding employment for farm workers where necessary.

Losses incurred as a result of forced sale of farming stock, furniture, etc would not be an admissible claim.

When the area was released from requisition in a similar manner, expenses reasonably incurred in moving furniture, etc., back would be reimbursed.

It was made clear that the act of requisition did not affect a tenant contract with his immediate landlord though any tenant could if he wished disclaim his tenancy provided the lease was terminable within five years of the date of requisition.

Unless for any reason the conditions of tenancy were broken, the tenant had the right to return to the property when the requisition order ended.

Landlords, farmers and owner-occupiers of cottages were advised to employ a professional agent to act for them in estimating any claim for compensation. The employment of an agent was permissible under any circumstances, but should not normally have been necessary where the claim for compensation was limited to garden produce, the cost of reasonable fees charged being reimbursed.

The farms on which claims for compensation have been made would be sent to everybody with the notices of requisition. It was important that these forms were properly completed before being returned to the admiralty lands officer. People were advised that the Admiralty lands officers would help anyone who did not know how to fill in the claim form.

Licences for Public Houses would not be extinguished by the requisition of the licensed premises. They would simply remain suspended and would come into force again after de-requisition.

A warning was issued that profiteering or any case of alleged profiteering, either in rent asked of persons leaving the area or in charges demanded for removal or storage, should be reported immediately at the information centre and, in the case of rents, to the local authority.

Representatives of the assistance board would visit all persons in receipt of supplementary pensions and would deal with any case where urgent financial assistance was required.

In relation to postal services, the Post Office would make arrangements for the prompt forwarding of letters, but everyone was advised to notify their changes of address to members of the family, especially to members serving in the forces.

A house-to-house delivery of redirection cards would be made. A list of Post Offices telephone exchanges and call offices to be closed, together with the name address and telephone number of the controlling head postmaster would be supplied to each information centre, and a map would also be supplied by the Post Office showing post offices and call offices still available just outside the area.

With regard to schools, children in elementary schools would go to the school in the town or village to which they moved. As there were no secondary schools in the area, it was hoped that it would be possible for any children at secondary schools to continue where their schools were situated or at the school boarding houses.

Any member of the Home Guard leaving the area was to report to his commanding officer for instructions before going. Likewise, special constables were to inform the nearest member of the regular police force of their intended movements.

Members of the civil defence services undertaking to join a corresponding service at their new home could take with them their personal equipment and on arrival were to report to the local head of the appropriate service.

It was recognised that the evacuation of whole communities would present many problems and many unforeseen difficulties. It was cautioned that people who resigned themselves to the necessity of removal as the result of enemy action might resent being disposed at the hands of their own government, and were therefore to be handled at all times with the greatest sympathy and tact.

It had been found in a similar case elsewhere that many people were in fact able to make arrangements for themselves and indeed preferred to do so, and where it was possible this was much the most satisfactory course. Therefore, except where otherwise recommended, people would be encouraged to act for themselves, and not given the impression that official assistance would be given with a grudging hand.

Commenting on the perceived way of the country folk living in the area, it was advised that a watch should always be kept for financial need and to remember that members of a country population might try to conceal their difficulties and would certainly be loath to accept anything which they regarded as state charity.

The evacuation would be an upheaval and a life-changing event for many. For the children involved it was seen as an adventure, for the adults involved the experiences differed in many ways. For the better off residents the problems were different to those of the farmers, shopkeepers and less well-off villagers.

Major Newman, the owner of Blackpool House near Stoke Fleming, had a large garden full of valuable tropical plants. He was able to enlist the assistance of his friend Mr Godfrey Nicholson MP to make enquiries on his behalf 'regarding the protection of certain interests'.[4]

The garden of the house was within the assault training area and he wished to know whether any arrangements could be made for safeguarding this valuable property from destruction through military training.

He was informed that troops undergoing training would be instructed to avoid damage to valuable and historic buildings particularly in the firing area. Any local civilians who wished to raise any complaint regarding their properties should do so through the regional commissioner South Western Area, General Sir Hugh Elles. It was suggested that Mr Nicholson should be informed on these lines.

Arrangements had in fact been made with the American Army Authorities for Blackpool House and grounds to be declared 'out of Bounds' to the troops using the area. It was not possible to exclude the property from the requisitioned area as it was within the danger area, though not in the target area, where no firing would take place.[5]

With regard to the preservation of the historic buildings within the area, arrangements where possible were put in place to safeguard them from damage.

In the case of the churches, arrangements had been made with the Bishop of Exeter personally for valuable fittings to be removed wherever possible and for other features to be protected. This work was carried out by experts and staff with considerable experience. The churches were extensively photographed for record purposes, by a naval photographer in conjunction with the Ministry of Works and the Diocesan Authorities.

Apart from the churches, two Roman camps and a few other buildings, it was regarded that there was little of architectural or historic interest within the area. The training area would be operated as a formal military range, and as such a formal set of Range Orders would be created. As part of these orders, provision was made for any buildings or features which the Ministry of Works deemed worthy of special protection, to be declared out of bounds to troops and vehicles using the area.

By mid-December, most people had moved from the area. The churches had been prepared for the worst with sandbags built up inside the walls and around the altars. The farms, villages and hamlets were largely deserted. Sir Hugh Elles reported that all the local agents of the government had done everything within their power to deal with the evacuation and had stretched the regulations to the limit. In addition he noted that the WVS had given much help, with representatives having travelled in excess of 105,000 miles in connection with evacuation work (T 161/1168).

Pinned to the door of Slapton Church was a message signed by the Bishop of Exeter. It read:

TO OUR ALLIES OF THE USA
The church has stood here for several hundred years. Around it has grown a community, which has lived in these houses and tilled these fields ever since there was a church. This church, this churchyard, in which their loved ones lie at rest, these homes, these fields, are as dear to those who have left them as are the homes and graves and fields which you, our Allies, have left behind you. They hope to return one day, as you hope to return to yours, to find them waiting to welcome them home. They entrust them to your care meanwhile and pray that God's blessing may rest upon us all.

Charles, Bishop of Exeter

The South Hams area has always had a slightly mystical quality, with its ancient woods and secluded valleys having changed little for hundreds of years. With the area now evacuated, this mystical quality was now further enhanced by an eerie silence that fell over the area. The silence, however, would not last for long. The Americans were about to arrive.

*Chapter Nine*

# Training for D-Day: Preparing and Planning

Using the experiences gained in previous amphibious operations, a conference was held over the period 24 May to 23 June 1943 at the Assault Training Centre at Woolacombe in North Devon to 'collect, assemble and evaluate as much as possible different uncorrelated factual data on assault landings; from actual experiences, studies of landings operation and other sources'.[1]

The Assault Training Centre, commanded by US Army Colonel Paul W. Thompson, was located on the North Devon coast, facing the Atlantic off the Bristol Channel. It had been set up to control and provide facilities for training of combat teams and assault divisions.

The training was designed to cover all phases of the landing–assault operation, under realistic conditions, simulating as closely as possible those to be encountered in the actual invasion itself. The centre would also be used for experimenting and testing new assault methods, and the development of tactics and techniques.

The area provided excellent conditions for beach assault training, with 8,000 yards of beaches, fronting on the ocean and 4,000 yards of beaches on a sheltered estuary. The hinterland behind the beaches ran to a depth of about 6,000 yards and was used for firing and manoeuvre. The beaches were flat and provided what was described as 'moderate' surf – thought to be probably stronger than that on the western coast of France. The beaches were similar to those of the Normandy beaches, and in order to simulate as closely as possible conditions there, the Devon beaches were fortified using German methods. These fortifications included bunkers, trenches, and mortar and gun positions. Large assault exercises were to be held here, as well as providing individual training for soldiers using specialist assault weapons and demolitions equipment. Training was also to be carried out to practice loading, unloading and assaulting from landing craft.

At the conference of May and June of 1943, British and US Officers discussed the best way to 'crack the nut' of Hitler's Atlantic Wall. The plan was to ensure that the latest developments were incorporated in the planning of the assault operations and that the most advanced training methods were used. The aim was to ensure that troops were properly trained and 'knew what they are doing and where they are going'.[2]

The training was to ensure that those who had not been involved in an actual operational landing would experience as broad a picture as possible and understand thoroughly what they were up against. The need to have well trained combat teams was recognised and the value of team spirit emphasised. The planned cross channel attack that was to take place would be on a scale never before attempted against a heavily defended coast.

Attending the Conference were:

Lt Gen Jacob L. Devers, Commanding General ETOUSA

Col P.W. Thompson, Commandant, Assault Training Center

Lt Col L.P. Chase (Chairman)

Maj Gen J.C Haydon (British), Vice Chief Combined Operations

Commodore J. Hughes-Hallett (RN), Naval Force commander at Dieppe

Maj Gen Hamilton Roberts (Canadian), Military Force Commander Dieppe Operation

Brigadier O.M. Wales (British), Commander 163rd Infantry Brigade

Lt Col R.O. Bare USMC, Combined Planning Staff

Lt Col C.R. Kutz, G-5 Section ETOUSA

Lt Col H.M. Zeller, Chief, Order of Battle Section, G-2 ETOUSA

Lt Col Bell Burton (British), GS01, British Army Intelligence

Col J.T. Dalbey, CoS Airborne Command

Maj Gen P.C. Hobart (British), General Officer Commanding, 79th Armoured Division

Col E.P. Lock, Engineer School, Ft Belvoir, VA

Col M.W. Brewster, Chief, Tactics Sub-Section, Assault Training Centre

Col H.F.G. Langley (British), Deputy Director of Experimental and Operational Requirements, Combined Headquarters

Brig Gen N.D. Cota, Chief of Combined Operations ETOUSA
Col H.H. Cleaves, Army Section, Amphibious Force, Atlantic Fleet
Col H.W. Grant, Air Signal Officer, Combined Operations
Maj A.G. Pixton, Services Sub-Section, Assault Training Centre
Col C.B. Spruit, Deputy Chief Surgeon, SOS, ETO
Col M.C. Grow, Surgeon, Eighth Air Force
Lt Col R. Adams, Training Branch, G-3 Div, WDGS
Lt Col A.T. Mason, USMC

In his address to the conference Brigadier General Norman Cota, Chief of Combined Operations ETOUSA, an experienced infantryman, clearly set out the challenges that lay ahead by stating that 'confusion and chaos are inherent in the very nature of the operation. Our every aim must be to overcome these inherent difficulties by careful honest and simple planning. In an operation of the kind we are considering our infantrymen before they can match their skill against the infantrymen of the foe, must compete against all elements of mother nature. If these are conquered they must then pass through man-made obstacles covered by expertly conceived concentrations of steel, smoke and fire.'[3]

He emphasised the fact that plans must be based on experience and that in operations of this nature it would be expected that errors will be made in navigation; there would be confusion during the landing and there would be interruptions in the landing program.

The conference featured a number of presentations. These included detailing operations from a historical perspective from both an offensive and defensive perspective. Specific subjects included: Combined Operations, the Naval Aspect of Dieppe, and The Defence of France and the Low Countries.

Referring directly to the Dieppe operation it was recognised that there had been a number of problems with the planning and execution of this operation. It had originally been planned for 20 June 1942 but had to be postponed twice, first to July then to August. This was as a result of naval training not having been complete. The five weeks originally planned for this training had been woefully insufficient.

Another problem was identified as having been the lack of common doctrine between land, sea and air forces. There had been no rigid timescale for the assault – this had depended on the tanks of the assaulting forces defeating the beach defences. No satisfactory decentralising system for naval command had existed. This resulted in the main command structure being inundated. The failure of the assault operation had necessitated a withdrawal based on a completely different plan than originally defined. It was recognised that this was achieved by the small number of experienced regular naval officers present on the operation.

The lessons learned from this operation were that:

- Much stronger forces are needed to break through the stronger parts of the German fortifications on the coast of France
- Intensive preparations by means of air and sea bombardment are essential in order to soften defences
- Much heavier support on a carefully organised basis is needed by the troops during the early phases of landing
- The military plan must be flexible because the bulk of military force must not be committed in the advance to any particular time or place of landing but must be held as a floating reserve ready to exploit success

Arising from the need to have flexible plan, a very much higher standard of training and organisation was needed on the part of the landing craft flotillas than had previously been thought necessary.

Specific aspects of amphibious operations in general were also covered, with The Support of a Landing Assault Operation, Airborne Troops in a Landing Assault, Armoured Fighting Vehicles in a Landing Assault, Artillery in a Landing Assault, Infantry in a Landing Assault, Signal Communications in a Landing Assault, Air Aspect of Communications, Chemical Warfare, Supply and Administration During a Landing Assault, Medical Service in a Landing Assault, Air Aspect Medical, Combined Arms in a Landing Assault, and Field Exercises. Major General Percy Hobart, commander of the British 79th Armoured Division, equipped with British designed specialist assault armour, also addressed the conference. He gave 'an unrecorded address on tanks' as it was recorded in the conference report. The actual content, which included a briefing on Swimming DD Tanks was deemed too secret at the time to be recorded within the report. Other topics also included German defence doctrine, defensive dispositions and the Reduction of Obstacles and Fortifications.

From the topics covered, it is possible to gain an understanding of the level of complication involved in the planning and preparation for the forthcoming assault and the level of detail and amount of thought that was to be invested in both the planning and the training.

The opening address clearly stated what had to be achieved: an invasion starting from the United Kingdom and having as its goal the enemy occupied coastline of Western Europe.

It was recognised that there were many different categories of responsibility, but the assault phase – the job of getting ashore – was the most difficult. It was also recognised that an operation of this scale and complication had never before in modern history taken place against such a strongly fortified coast. The history of the United Kingdom was cited to testify the difficulty of the problem. A cross channel operation had been the dream of many great soldiers. Napoleon had the idea but was not properly organised to accomplish it. Hitler had also had the same idea but failed to undertake it. They had both faced tremendous difficulties and it was safe to assume that it was just as much of a task to head towards the continent as towards England. The English Channel had long proved to be a fierce no-man's-land. Its short distance across had been a misleading factor to many would-be invaders.

The fundamental problem was to get across the Channel with properly organised assault teams, and to seize and hold a beachhead through which could pour a strategic force.

It was recognised that for this operation, whilst it could be guided by existing tactical doctrine, there would be specific needs to be catered for that would not have been encountered before. The task of training for this was what lay ahead of them. Having open minds and a willingness to formulate new tactical doctrine was vital. Modern history provided no satisfactory precedent for the specific and unique type of operation that involved crossing the English Channel.

A wealth of information existed from previous operations in the form of uncorrelated factual data, experiments, and actual experiences in landing operations, but this needed to be assembled into a useable form to produce a sound and comprehensive new doctrine.

The function of the conference was to collate, evaluate and finally to assemble this data in a form suitable for use by the assault training centre as training doctrine. The training centres specific mission was that of training divisions and their subordinate units for the assault of a heavily fortified coast as a preliminary to a cross channel invasion.

Major General J.C. Haydon DSO and Bar, Vice Chief of Combined Operations, a proven operational commander in the field and a brilliant staff officer, addressed the gathering: 'I think I can define the assault by saying that it means putting ashore at the right time and at the right place fighting units in fighting order under an integrated fire plan and with a regulated follow up coming along behind. Easy to say but not easy to do.'

He went on to describe how to successfully achieve an amphibious operation along with the problems of doing so. First of all there was a need for speed. The assault in broad terms would be a race between trains and vehicles across the continent and boats across the Channel where it was vital to ensure that the build-up of assaulting forces kept pace with the rate of reinforcement by the enemy.

It was acknowledged that Germans, so far as could be judged from aerial photography, seemed to rely on their coastal defences, which were extremely strong. The physical difficulties that these provided were very considerable indeed. The Germans pinned their faith on absolutely solid concrete defences which in some cases included anti-tank walls some 8 to 10 yards high and 8 to 10 yards thick. In addition there were anti-tank ditches, minefields, and wire, with carefully concealed well-placed searchlights ready to light up the beaches. Their defensive doctrine was based on delaying the initial landing to give them time to counter-attack as well as giving time for reinforcements to arrive and to prevent the assault force properly deploying. However, it was also recognised that despite these elaborate and strong defensive systems, the Germans also had weaknesses. They had severe manpower problems; they were short of men for the very great number of tasks that confronted them. They could not therefore strongly hold every beach on the coast because they simply didn't have the men to do it.

Accuracy of intelligence relating to the rate of arrival and the proportion of armour and infantry that could be expected was also deemed to be vital, as was an accurate estimation of the enemy's air threat. Taking all these factors into account would give the final judgment as to what type of plan was required.

Then there was the English Channel itself. The crossing was long and the weather changeable at all times of the year. It was recognised that soldiers in landing craft would probably suffer from sickness, and although they would recover quickly, it would be hard to predict how fit they would be at the moment they touched down on the beach. Some might go on feeling indisposed for some time, but all who had been ill would automatically lose some of their stamina.

Most of the landing craft available at that time could operate under adverse conditions, but there would be a need for sheltered or alternative anchorages to allow continuous uninterrupted discharge of men, vehicles and supplies over the beaches. If a successful landing could be made, and if the weather broke after the assault had been made the forces ashore would have to be continuously supplied with more materiel.

The need for ports and harbours was be urgent. During the last similar landings, during Operation Torch the Allied invasion of North Africa, the ports of Algiers, Oran and Casablanca had been captured early.

The provision of direct fire support during the landing phase was discussed in some detail. Direct close fighter support was identified as a definite requirement. Not only did this provide practical support, it also slowed the rate of enemy reinforcement, had a major effect on supplies of materiel, and also on morale and the enemy's will to fight. It could not however give prolonged help during the moment of the assault, due to the danger to friendly forces. At this time its direction would need to be focused on targets that lay inland or away from the landing places.

Direct fire support for the landing force by the navy was recognised as being difficult due to the fact that the ships were standing too far out to sea to effectively support the assaulting land forces during the beach assault. The distance made supporting ships remote from the immediate tactical needs of the troops ashore.

Experience of this had been gained at Dieppe and this was referred to again. The availability and effectiveness of bombardment by high explosive and smoke had been regarded as ineffective on this operation. Some close support had been available from the 4-inch guns of the naval force, but something much bigger such as that from 12-inch guns was recommended. Ideally this would be delivered at point blank range and some form of armoured monitor was suggested as the solution for this.

For support craft going in with the first assault wave, firepower provided by 20mm Oerlikon cannon or .50 calibre heavy machine guns were judged to be sufficient above sea level to give close range overhead support during the actual process of disembarking. It was considered that even heavier guns should be made available: two pounder or preferably 40mm guns.

A wider question was asked regarding the use of parachute or other airborne troops and should they be included in the operation. The answer was a resounding Yes!

The training for those taking part in the actual assault was particularly focused on the squad leaders and platoon leaders. The more training spent at this level, it was felt, the greater the gain would be. It was at this level that in the expected chaos of an opposed beach landing, decisions would need to be made.

The training was to be comprehensive and long, would weed out poor leaders, and would become tedious for many taking part but 'they will thank you for it on D-Day when they go ashore'.[4]

The discussions that took place regarding the assault itself covered the merits and types of assault craft and naval supporting fire, the importance of obstacle clearing by engineer troops, and the types of weapons available to counter these obstacles.

The composition of the US assault forces would be based around a three battalion US Infantry Regiment. Acknowledging that this was the case, but also that the assaulting force would include a number of organic supporting troops, the title Regimental Combat Team (RCT) was adopted.

The RCT would comprise:

An Infantry Regiment
A Field Artillery Battalion
Two batteries of AA artillery
A single platoon of reconnaissance troops
A signal detachment
A medical collecting company

An ordnance detachment
Special communication and liaison groups for naval and air liaison
Engineer battalions
A medical battalion

A Beach Group would also be part of the assault forces. This group would be made up of specialists and include QM service battalions, QM gas supply companies, ordnance ammunition detachments, ordnance medium maintenance companies, MP companies, amphibian truck companies, chemical decontamination companies, detachment group regulating station transport corps troops, QM railhead companies. These troops all had specific skills that allowed them to support and supply the initial landing and the follow–up divisions. They would be responsible for controlling the beach area so that the troops and supplies could pass through in the most expeditious manner and would be required to land early in the operation.

Naval Beach parties would also land in first assault wave. They would set up range markers in the centre of the beach to guide the boats of the following waves, then assist in guiding boats to the correct beaches.

All these supporting troops needed to be trained for combat and would be married to and train with the assault divisions which they were to support.

Having provided a thorough and detailed walkthrough of the multitude of subjects that would make up the forthcoming assault, the conference concluded with a look back at how it had done and concluded that there was an 'intangible, although priceless ingredient – the fact that officers of the Army, Navy and Air Forces of Great Britain and the United States worked together, side-by-side, regardless of uniform or service, motivated by the same aim, the same goal'. This goal was the successful invasion of Nazi Occupied Europe and for those taking part in the assault this spirit of cooperation would be vital to ensure both the survival and success of those taking part.

*Chapter Ten*

# The Exercises

The exercises that took place at Slapton Sands, Blackpool Sands and the hinterland beyond, were designed to fulfil a number of requirements. The primary uses were for practice and rehearsals for assault units, and logistic support as part of the necessary support and follow-up involved in an assault landing.

As there were to be a number of new tactics and procedures used as part of Operation Overlord, these had to be experimented with, tested and practiced to ensure that everything worked, and also to create necessary procedures that did not yet exist.

The actual assault was of course the key to a successful assault landing, but the precursors of marshalling, embarking and transporting thousands of troops were also major undertakings. The men had to be assembled, concentrated, and loaded onto ships and landing craft. During the pre-assault phase they had to be accommodated, fed and looked after to ensure that they would be fit and capable of performing efficiently in the assault. This was to be a mammoth task, and all had to be practiced.

The units taking part went through a structured training program. Starting with basic soldiering skills, they would train first at the lowest sub-unit level, then as a larger unit (e.g. regiment), then in full-scale rehearsals as a complete assault formation. During this training they would also undertake specialist assault training at the Assault Training Center at Woolacombe, which provided another key training facility allowing troops to practice working with landing craft, train with specialist assault weapons and train collectively as units in the assault.

Constant practice in driving army vehicles on and off landing vessels was performed. All army personnel engaged in working with army equipment while being loaded onto, carried in, or discharged from naval vessels, were given sound practice over many months. Likewise, naval personnel required to handle army equipment during operation were given specialised practice in doing so. Strictly naval training in boat operation, beaching and retracting, discharging cargo into 'ferry craft' from large ships, and all other aspects of amphibious duties were also carried out during the pre-assault period.

The Slapton Sands area provided the environment in which to build on all the unit and specialist training, and allowed large formations to practice together.

## The Slapton Sands Training Area

The training area and range at Slapton Sands was set up and run on the same basis as a traditional Army Training Area. A set of Range Standing Orders were created and a Range Party set up to run the training area. The Range Commandant was a Colonel Martleing who had his headquarters at Ash House, near Blackawton.

The range party was responsible for:

- Ensuring barricades were placed across all roads leading into the area (sentries were placed at the Frogmore and Stoke Fleming barricades. Units using other roads were instructed to replace barricades or post sentries during time the barricade was open)
- Making the necessary arrangements to keep unauthorised persons outside the boundaries of the area at all times
- The correct posting of all sentries and the withdrawal of sentries on completion of firing where necessary
- Carrying out repairs to roads and bridges which had been damaged and informing of damage to property
- When exercises were due to take place, responsible for range clear and safety arrangements
- Erection of danger flags – to be hoisted by range party
- Provisions of patrols (nine patrols of one man each were required to cover the perimeter of eighteen miles)
- Repair of targets (this applied only to permanent and semi-permanent targets. Other targets were required to be repaired by the units providing them)

- Upkeep of roads and property
- Putting out small isolated fires if no unit was using the range for those unable to deal with assistance called for from local US fire fighting units
- Salvage of metal
- Cooking (cooks were provided to cook food for twenty-five sentries as well as for the range party)
- Ensuring that red flags were hoisted on range boundaries, that posts and flags ashore marked the impact area for guns, and that transit marks were erected to show the shore limits of impact area for guns afloat.

With regard to Live Firing taking place from seaward and onshore, a clear set of safety instructions were issued:

- Anti-tank guns and armour piercing ammunition were not to be used. Practice ammunition (US term 'solid shot') was also not to be used
- Limitations of firing and safety precautions (units afloat). The impact area for guns afloat was approximately 3,000 yards inside the range boundary. No round was to be aimed outside the impact area. In addition an area on the foreshore could be used for direct fire from seaward
- The angle of descent and direction of fire was to be arranged so that projectiles or ricochets were not liable to fall outside the range boundary.

The firing officer in the unit afloat was responsible for seeing that these safety precautions were observed.

Limitations of firing and safety precautions were specified for bombing and machine gun strafing by aircraft. Bombing was to be restricted to targets in the 'units afloat' impact area and bombs larger than 600lb demolition were not to be used.

Pyrotechnic light signals were arranged and orders distributed to range users in case it was necessary to stop firing when exercises were taking place.

A shore firing control party was to be provided by the US naval unit or HM ships taking part in the exercise. This was to be done in accordance with instructions issued by the range commandant.

The officer in charge of the shore firing control party was responsible for:

- Providing communication between ship and shore
- Advising the senior officer afloat at least thirty minutes before firing commenced, that the range was clear. This information was to be obtained from the range commandant who was also to be informed when the firing practice was complete
- Passing 'Cease Fire' if for any reason the range became foul
- Providing observations on fall of shot if required.

As with all ranges where live firing takes place it was necessary to search for unexploded bombs, grenades and shells (US term 'duds'). On completion of all exercises a thorough search for duds of all types would be instituted by the range commandant. Located duds were to be blown up in the presence of an officer. An area in which unlocated duds were suspected was to be reported at the conclusion of firing to the range commandant. Such areas were be marked on the ground by the range commandant until the duds had been destroyed. All troops using the range were to be warned to look out for duds and report their location to an officer who was to report to the range commandant.

No firing was to occur unless properly scheduled. Unauthorised firing had previously been cause for alarm on the part of other troops training in the area and also workmen in the area.

The exercises that took place at Slapton Sands can be divided into three groups.

The first were the early major exercises involving troops from several units working together on combined assault and supply problems. In these exercises the various phases of the invasion were covered, including mounting, landing and consolidation of the beachhead.

The second group consisted of smaller exercises participated in by individual units training for their own particular phase of the invasion.

The third group consisted of dress rehearsals.

All major American formations that took part in the Assault on Utah and Omaha beaches trained at Slapton Sands. The first of a series of large-scale amphibious exercises, Exercise Duck took place between 31 December and 2 January 1944. From then on almost continual exercises were held at Slapton Sands. Altogether three Duck exercises were held (Duck I, II and III) and involved assault units scheduled to land on Omaha Beach.

A view of the Slapton beach area taken from the high ground above Torcross. The freshwater lake known as Slapton Ley can be seen behind the beach. *(Jim Linwood)*

A view approaching the beach at Slapton Sands taken from the sea. This would have been the view seen by the troops as they approached the beach. *(Authors Collection)*

RAIDING FORCES OF "EASTLAND" MAKE A LANDING ON SLAPTON SANDS.

A newspaper report showing the 1938 practice assault landings. Five years later, once again the beach at Slapton Sands would be used for assault exercises but for a real war and on a much larger scale. *(Authors collection)*

Men of the Durham Light Infantry practice bayonet fighting on the beach at Slapton in Devon, 30 August 1940. *(IWM H3551)*

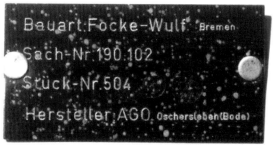

The makers' plate recovered from Oblt Laumann's FW 190. *(Chris Goss)*

A picture of Oblt Oswald Laumann, the tip and run raider shot down and killed on 23 March 1943 at Strete. *(The Aircrew Remembrance society – Adam Lewis )*

This remarkable photo shows a tip and run raid taking place – the target is Torcross. The photo is taken from the cockpit by Lt Leopold Wenger in one of the attacking FW190's. *(Chris Goss)*

A group of Luftwaffe officers and pilots pictured in front of an aircraft belonging to II/SKG 10 – Laumann's unit. Laumann's FW 190 aircraft was coded 'H' the aircraft in this picture is coded 'G'. *(Chris Goss)*

Troops coming ashore during an exercise. An M7 105 mm self-propelled howitzer can also be seen on the beach. *(Photos Normandie)*

American LCTs beached on the shingle at Slapton Sands. The officer in the foreground wearing a white armband is acting as an exercise umpire. *(Photos Normandie)*

US M10 Motor Gun Carriage Tank destroyers come ashore at Slapton Sands. In the background LST 325 can be seen. LST 325 is still in existence, and is preserved in the United States. *(Photos Normandie)*

An iconic photo showing men coming ashore on the beach at Slapton Sands. The unit is unknown but may possibly be a headquarters of specialist unit as they are all armed with M1 Carbines rather than the standard M! Garand Service rifle issued to men of rifle companies. *(Photos Normandie)*

This photo shows the centre of the beach area during an exercise. In the background the remains of the Royal Sands Hotel can be seen smoking, possibly as a result of being hit during a preliminary bombardment. *(Photos Normandie)*

This photo shows Canadian soldiers embarking at Slapton Sands during Exercise Trousers. *(Authors Collection)*

A group of senior officers pictured at Slapton Sands during Exercise Trousers. From left to right in the foreground, Admiral Ramsay the naval commander for Operation 'Overlord' ; Brigadier H.W. Foster the commanding officer of the 7th Canadian Infantry Brigade ; Admiral Philip Vian, commander of Force J; General Bernard Montgomery commander 21st Army Group; and General Miles Dempsey commander of the Second Army. *(US National Archive)*

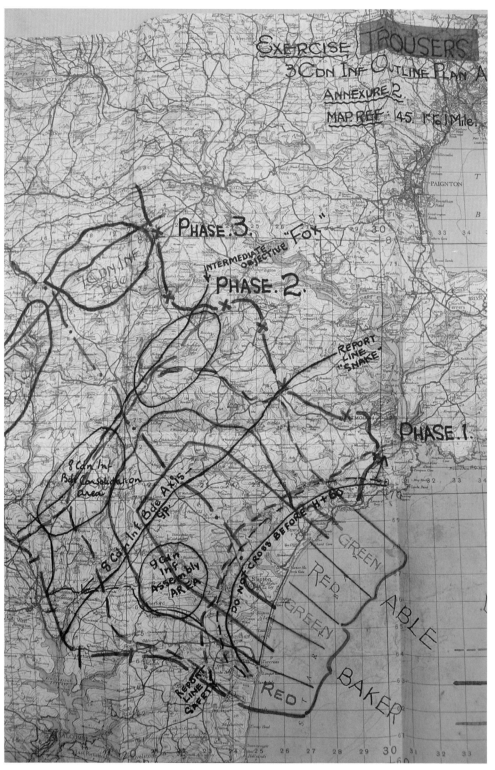

An original map showing the landing beaches and objective for Exercise Trousers. *(Authors Collection)*

US troops performing an assault exercise at Blackpool Sands. A much smaller and separate beach to Slapton Sands, it was just within the requisitioned area and also used during the assault exercises. *(Authors Collection)*

US troops landing at Slapton Sands during what is believed to be Exercise Fabius I. *(US National Archive)*

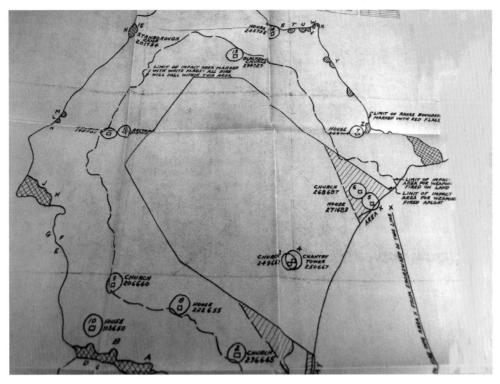

An Exercise Fabius map overlay of the Slapton Sands and hinterland area. The area behind the beach designated as the impact area can clearly be seen as well as the various areas marked as not to be fired on within the impact area itself. *(Authors Collection)*

The Sherman DD tank recovered from the sea off Slapton Sands in 1984. *(Authors Collection)*

This picture shows an exercise taking place at Slapton Sands. Behind the half-track in the foreground a DD tank be seen with it screen lowered. *(US National Archive)*

A DD tank operating at sea. *(Authors Collection)*

Another picture of a Sherman DD tank. In this picture the canvas flotation screen and propellers located at the rear of the vehicle can clearly be seen. *(Authors Collection)*

Pictured after the finish of the exercises, this picture is looking west on the A379 heading towards Slapton Sands. The badly damaged buildings on the right were subsequently knocked down and turned into a car park. *(IWM D31956)*

This picture, taken in September 1944, highlights the danger of anti-personnel mines still present. This would have been before the civil population returned to the area, so is probably a warning to those performing the clear-up operations. *(IWM D21973)*

The memorial at Slapton Sands to commemorate those that so generously gave up their homes to allow the training to take place at Slapton Sands. *(Authors Collection)*

One of the bunkers located above the beach at the Strete Gate end of Slapton Sands. Pictured in the 1990s it still clearly showed the damage from shellfire resulting from the assault exercises in 1944. It has been subsequently demolished. *(Authors Collection)*

The beach pictured in the 1980s. Erosion has subsequently pushed the beach back towards the road. *(Authors Collection)*

A Landing Craft Tank Rocket – LCT (R) – firing a salvo of rockets. These were used during the exercises at Slapton Sands. *(Wikimedia Commons)*

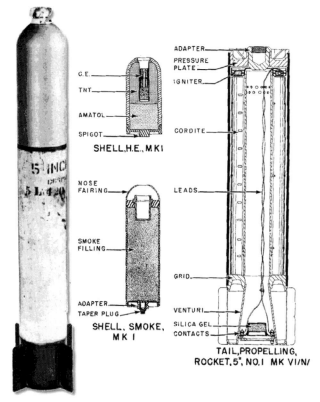

A diagram of a British 5" High Explosive rocket as fired by the LCT (R). Many of the items of unexploded ordnance uncovered over the years are examples of this type of rocket. *(Authors Collection)*

A selection of smaller artefacts discovered at Slapton Sands. These include spent cartridge cases, shell fragments and bullets. *(Authors Collection)*

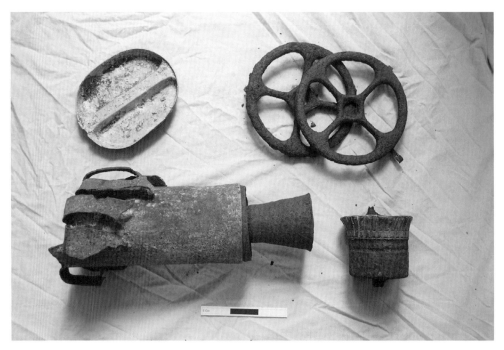

A selection of larger artefacts discovered at Slapton Sands. These include (top left) the top half of an American soldiers mess tin, (top right) parts of American M1A1 anti-tank mines, (bottom right) the remains of a detonated British 5" Rocket, and (bottom left) part of an exploded 42 Naval projectile. *(Authors Collection)*

Exercise Fox, which took place over the period 9–10 March also involved units scheduled to assault Omaha Beach.

Exercise Fabius I took place in early May 1944 and provided the final dress rehearsal for Force 'O'.

Units of the 4th Infantry Division and the 1st Engineer Special Brigade which were to assault Utah Beach, also undertook a series of exercises designed to give experience to all 4th Division assault units and to the D-Day elements of the 1st Engineer Special Brigade. These comprised two major exercises – Exercise Beaver in March 1944 and Exercise Tiger in April 1944.

Additionally, the 3rd Canadian Infantry Division that would assault Juno Beach also performed a major rehearsal at Slapton Sands.

A number of smaller exercises were carried out and also exercises to practice and test the logistic beachhead supply processes.

The exercises were multi-faceted and complex, involving thousands of men and vehicles and hundreds of ships. Naval gunfire support, ground attack by aircraft, and simulated airborne landings were also included. Every effort was made to duplicate actual battle conditions. Records of these operations only exist in partial detail for separate exercises. The following account hopefully pieces together details for all the major elements, spread over different exercises:

## Exercise Duck

This was the first major exercise mounted at Slapton Sands. The assault was made by elements of the 29th Infantry Division, part of the US V Corps. Naval bombardment was carried out by four Royal Navy Hunt class destroyers who, together with trawlers and minesweepers, acted as escort during the passage and while the assault forces were in the area. In this and in later exercises, all bombarding ships and escorts were placed under the direct operational control of the Assault Force Commander, while covering forces of destroyers and coastal craft remained under the operational control of Commander-in-Chief, Plymouth. Exercise Duck was a training operation involving a concentration, embarkation at more than one point, sea movement, debarkation, and an assault of an occupied beach area with a seizure of an objective inland. The purpose of the exercise was to train the units involved in planning and executing the various phases of an amphibious operation involving a landing on a hostile shore.

Exercise Duck marked the beginning of the process of assigning vessels and amphibious parties their assault organisation. Rear-Admiral Hall (commander of the 11th Amphibious Force) followed the policy of 'marrying-up' the naval and army units as early as possible so that the army-naval personnel and commanders on all echelons would be able to work and train together for as long as possible. This could not be done all at one time, since not all the army formations nor all the navy vessels were available at so early a date, while those that were available had to be inter-changed so as to give training to all. Despite these handicaps the process of making definite assignments began early and proceeded as rapidly as the arrival of forces would allow.

### Exercise Duck I

Duck I was the first of the major exercises and probably the most important, since the flaws shown up by it greatly affected training and planning of the following exercises. Plans for Duck I were discussed as early as mid-summer 1943, but the actual planning did not begin until early November. It was first conceived as a mounting exercise for Services of Supply, but ultimately was extended to other units so that it included all phases of an assault landing. The actual decision to hold Duck I was made on 21 November 1943. The exercise was broken into two phases. The first was concentration, processing and embarkation of assault troops, and the second was the actual assault. Following embarkation of the units, the 11th Amphibious Force was to move the troops from the embarkation point to the assault beach and, with the help of British naval units, protect the convoy from any attacks by German submarines and E-boats. Troops for the assault were embarked at Falmouth and Dartmouth. To prevent damage to embarkation points, the 'sausage' plan, under which assembly areas were built around secondary paved roads, was developed. The roads were blocked off to all civilian traffic and were used as hard standings. Tents were located along the edge of the roads in wooded areas. Because of the shape of the areas on maps, they were nicknamed 'sausages'. The success of this plan not only made other exercises possible, but also was adopted during the real D-Day operations. The first

informal meeting of the Duck I staff was held on 24 November at XIX
District headquarters near Taunton. It was decided that the exercise would
be held in daylight because of safety factors and to facilitate observation.
The following day Major General Henry M. Gerow, commanding general of
V Corps, accepted the proposals. The development of the detailed plan, the
construction of installations, and the assembling of supplies and personnel
followed immediately. Activities in the first phase included planning,
constructing and assembling troops and supplies, marrying the various
auxiliary units to combat teams, processing troops from concentration areas
through marshalling areas, movement from marshalling areas to 'hards'[1],
loading the landing craft at the hards, preparation, loading and dispatch of
coasters, protection of evacuated villages from assault fire, transportation
and feeding of troops on their return from the assault area, and transporting
them to their home stations. A total of 553 officers and 9,603 enlisted men
were required to perform the Service of Supply (SOS) functions in the
exercise.

The following assault troops and vehicles participated in Duck I:

Adv Hq V Corps
29th Inf Div (minus 2 RCT's)
1st Engr Spec Brig
Hq & Hq Btry, 3rd Tank Gp
741st Tank Bn
803rd TD Bn
634th AAA Awpns Bn
Co C 81st Cml Bn (Mtz)
56th Sig Bn
Hq & HQ Btry 76th FA Brig
203rd MP Co
Co D 466th QM Trk Regt
CIC Det V Corps
668th Engr Topo Co
15th Bomb Disp Sqd
Hq & Hq Det & Med Det 177th Ord Bn
4th Plat 506th AM Car Co

Elements of Service of Supply Troops
Elements of IX USAAF
Elements of US Navy

Embarkation took place from D-6 to D-1 from the ports of Falmouth and Dartmouth. Landing craft involved comprised 14 LSTs, 34 LCTs, 5 LCMs and 161 LCVPs comprising the Falmouth assault force and 57 LCMs forming the Dartmouth assault force. The sea journey began prior to D-Day, and was to take place at Slapton Sands, which was assumed to be a section of the coast of Western Europe.

As this exercise was a precursor to many more, the capacities for the various types of landing craft were tested in various configurations. These included LCTs which were loaded as follows:

- 6x1½ ton 6x6 trucks, 6x57mm AT guns, 3x¼ ton trucks. It was noted that these could be loaded in 30 minutes. Trailers were backed in while coupled in normal position and considerable difficulty was experienced guiding them on.
- 6x2½ ton 6x6 trucks, 4x40mm AA guns, 2x¼ ton trucks. These could be loaded in 25 minutes. Trailers were winched on by first truck loaded in centre at stern and manhandled into position. This method was deemed to be much more efficient.
- 5x2½ ton 6x6 trucks, 4x105mm howitzers, 3x¼ ton trucks.
- Ammunition for offshore firing was also loaded. Gun trails were lashed to front tow hooks of trucks; trucks were backed on to decks towing guns. Trails of the two bow guns, which were to fire, were then spread and lashed to the deck.
- 2x M25 tank recovery truck tractors, 3xTD 18 tractors, 1xT2 tank recovery unit, 1x2½ amphibian truck.
- Additional loadings included: 1 medium tank in an LCM, 5 medium or 7 to 8 light tanks in LCT and 60 to 70 vehicles in LST.

The general plan was to embark the 29th Infantry Div (less two regimental combat teams) reinforced with 1st Engineer Special Brigade, Hq & Battery, 3rd Tank Group, 741st Tank Battalion (M), 803rd Tank Destroyer Battalion,

634th AAA Air Weapons Battalion, and a Naval Beach Battalion in the Falmouth and Dartmouth areas. They were to move under control of the US Navy, disembark, and with Navy and Air support assault the beach between the road junction and the raised beach southeast of Slapton and Pilchard Cove, with assumed landings on Blackpool Beach and south of Slapton during daylight at H–Hour on D–Day, to secure the general line inland along the Dittisham–Moreleigh road and to cover the landing of the 28th Infantry Division (assumed).

A secondary assault by a Ranger Battalion was assumed to have taken place against Coleton Heights (approximately 3.5 miles to the east) to contain enemy forces in the Brixham Peninsula and delay enemy observation from Coleton Heights.

Land elements of the IX USAAF and Advanced Hq V Corps would also be embarked on the beach in the vicinity of Manor House (south of Strete) behind the 29th Infantry Division.

D–Day was Monday, 3 January 1944.

The assault phase of the exercise went largely according to schedule. There was a bombardment of the beach prior to H–Hour to reduce obstacles and strong points and at 10:00 hours the first units came ashore. The actual assaulting troops consisted of a reinforced infantry regiment with two battalions in the assault and one in reserve. Live ammunition was used. Additional imaginary assaults were deemed to be occurring on each flank.

The landings did not go entirely according to plan, and some craft came ashore in the wrong wave, but by and large the landings were smooth. Enemy forces were entirely imaginary but included fourteen pillboxes, each with at least two machine guns, and there were eight machine guns in open emplacements. The southern part of one beach was assumed to have been mined. Three four-gun batteries of 105-mm howitzers and one two–gun battery of 150-mm howitzers were assumed to be behind the beach. There were anti-aircraft batteries, and one enemy airfield. Enemy capabilities included limited air, submarine and small surface-craft action, a defence at the beach line, a secondary defence along hastily prepared cliff lines, an armoured attack by elements of one panzer division by H+3 hours, another by two tank battalions and one armoured infantry regimental combat team at H+8 hours, and a third by a maximum of four infantry regimental combat teams after D+1. Pillboxes had been built and other defence works indicated by flags, and the assaulting troops were required by umpires to take some suitable action before passing them. There were no underwater obstacles. There was a continuous belt of wire (about three concertina-type rolls) extended along the seaward side of the highway which paralleled the beach about fifty yards from high water. Tubular steel frame obstacles interwoven with barbed wire were also present at some points on the assault beaches, but these were not extensive. A few very small minefields were said to be on the beaches, but these also were not extensive.

Slapton Ley, the inshore fresh-water lake lying behind the western side of the beach, which at its widest point is approximately 100 yards across, formed a serious natural obstacle. This caused a great deal of trouble, since bridging equipment failed to arrive in time. As the men went ashore, they assaulted the simulated pillboxes, blew them up, made their way inland and established defences. The 1st Engineer Special Brigade units began to land a H+25 minutes. They de-mined one beach, cleared the other, and set up three supply beaches. Beach exits were established, and unloading activities begun. In the afternoon of D-Day the coasters arrived and were unloaded by DUKWs and landing craft. Dumps were established inland, and a number of supply experiments were tried out. The Chemical Warfare Service tested new mobile decontamination equipment loading methods. The engineers tried out methods of track-laying to improve beach roads, tested amphibiously packed items, and carefully checked new waterproofing techniques. Quartermaster units continued their experiments with palletised loadings, and the Signal Corps set up a new system of loudspeakers for giving orders to troops and trucks in congested areas. Skid loading of signal equipment and amphibious packing were also tested.

On D+1 organisation of a beach maintenance area and landing supplies commenced. It was emphasised that the exercise was conducted entirely for the purpose of training, that it was neither a demonstration nor a test, that it would proceed at a deliberately retarded rate in order to facilitate training, and that several types of support (e.g. air, support and rocket craft) were omitted.

The exercise lasted two days, and then the troops were returned to their own stations.

Events of D–Day were observed from the visitor's observation post about three miles south of the actual landings. Some reports from the observers present, residing in the National Archives at Kew, are reproduced here:

The observers noted that the weather was cloudy with occasional light showers, making more detailed observation impossible. Events as they appeared from that distance were:

**H-90** (H being 1000 hours): A destroyer was seen close to the beach, followed very soon by another.

**H-77**: Destroyers started firing. First shots landed in the water, but were soon on the beach and the higher ground behind. Firing was with reduced charges and evidently in reduced volume also; it was not heavy. This fire was scheduled for H-1 to H-5. Craft were seen approaching about the time fire opened.

**H-45**: Small craft were announced to be assembling in rendezvous areas. They appeared to be headed toward the beach following larger naval vessels. They appeared to be in column until 0940 when first wave fanned out into a rough line or wedge formation.

**H-10**: First wave of small craft (Said to be LCVP) passed their guiding vessels. They seemed to be moving faster than before. Fire at this time was announced to be partly from FA mounted in LCT.

**H-Hour**: Eight craft landed on north beach, north of Manor House. They were said to be carrying part of two companies of right assault Bn. The craft put the troops almost on dry land. They were unloaded and headed back to sea within seconds. The troops deployed and remained for some time (about forty minutes) not more than fifty yards from the water. They appeared to form a vulnerable target. The reason for not advancing more rapidly is not known; they may have been waiting for gaps to be made in the wire.

**H-3 1003**: Smoke puffs, said to be white phosphorus grenades, appeared ahead of the troops on the beach, partly obscuring them from view. It seems likely that some of these puffs were Bangalore torpedoes in the wire.

**H+7**: About eight craft landed troops on the south beach south of Manor House. These were said to be part of left assault battalion seven minutes behind schedule. Two of the craft were stuck on the beach for some time. This Bn also remained near the unloading points for some time before advancing.

**H+20**: Support wave of right (north) Bn landed in about eight craft. These were said to include chemical mortars.

**H+30**: Eight additional small craft landed on north beach.

**H-42**: Troops could be seen crossing road behind north beach continuing on uphill across the fields.

**H+42**: Two LCM landed on the south beach, apparently carrying bulldozers and beach sleds. One unloaded at once. The other apparently had difficulty and did not unload until 1056. One bulldozer had disappeared, the other remained near the landing point.

**H+75**: Strete gate (assumed to be a road block – it was not seen) was blasted. The charge, 1000 lbs, had been placed in advance and was not brought in by craft. Smaller blasts continued to occur near the beach; their nature was not explained.

**H+77**: Troops of left assault Bn started moving across the road behind the south beach. By this time troops of the right Bn were moving across fields several hundred yards beyond the road. A flame-thrower appeared to be in use at one point about this time.

**H+ 80**: Another LCM landed on south beach, while on north beach about 2 LCM, 4 LCVP and 1 LCT landed.

**H+84:** Additional LCVP landed on north beach, followed closely by more on south beach.

**H+100:** Reserve Bn and some Engr troops landed in 8 LCI. Two LCI were away from the beach, except for 1, by 1155. The one remained stuck until 1210.

**H+150:** About eight LCT landed. Their contents could not be identified. Smaller craft continued to land in small numbers.

**H+185:** Additional LCT landed. Vehicles from the LCT appeared to be crossing beach to the road in rear and proceeding towards Strete. Some vehicles apparently were stuck in the sand, which was fairly coarse, but with neither larger material nor much fine material to bind it. It looked as if bulldozers were towing many vehicles.

**H+125:** Most of the troops were off the beach by this time. Additional LCT and LCI continued to land during the afternoon. It was announced that they were waiting off shore to come in as called. It was announced about 1500 that FA had not landed but was in LCT waiting to be called.

**1515:** An LST landed. No vehicles had been discharged when visitors departed at **1600**.

The exercise was watched by observers at an observation point on a hill southwest of Torcross. When the exercise had completed, the observers finished their note-taking, and began a series of critiques to discover the good and bad points of the exercise.

Some points raised in the after-action reports are included here:

**Navy:** Liaison in general needed improvement, particularly in regard to provisioning of craft. In general, naval participation could not be judged, since the Navy had very limited resources to draw upon for the exercise. Craft commanders, particularly of LSTs, did not appreciate the necessity of beaching at the proper points, and coordination between Army and Navy was generally lacking.

**Air Force**: The Air Force was unable to participate until D+1 when a few reconnaissance missions were flown. Air force supply troops were landed on the beach from different craft and had difficulty in reassembling.

**Planning**: Planning suffered because of the distance between planning agencies, and also because a planning staff was assembled very hurriedly. A combined planning group, centrally located, was suggested for future exercises. Phasing of planning was bad; for example, the embarkation plan was finished late and held up other phases of the operation.

**Mounting**: Better pre-packaging of freight, improved transportation flexibility and an improved conservation of transportation was called for. Movement of troops and supplies was slow, but it was evident that it could easily be stepped up in the future.

**Concentration areas**: Most of the troops involved were already stationed near enough to embarkation points to complete concentration in their home stations. Units were fully equipped and manned and organised into craft parties with proper scale of equipment (assault or light).

**Assembly areas:** These were elongated areas laid out axially along a road for a distance of about 6 miles the area being 5 to 10 miles from embarkation points. Four areas served the Falmouth embarkation sector. Each contained 14 tented camps and capacity for parking 2,000 vehicles. One area, containing 4 camps and 200 vehicle parking capacity, served the Dartmouth area. Capacity of a camp was 200 troops, who normally remained there for 4 to 12 hours. Meals were provided and each tent contained 6 cots provided with 4 blankets and a candle. Tent stoves and fuel were provided.

Five camp areas were set aside for the exercise. Four of them, A, B, C and D, were located in the Falmouth-Helston-Redruth-Lanviet-St Austell-Truro area, and the fifth, Camp Area E, was located at Lupton House, East Dartmouth. Each camp consisted of 41 squad tents for living purposes; 1 squad tent served as headquarters and supply tent; field kitchens; a 1-hospital ward tent for dining tent. Pit latrines were utilised. Tents were heated with M41 stoves. Water and gasoline were delivered daily by tank trucks, which stopped to fill 5-gallon cans stocked at each camp. One telephone was available in each headquarters tent. Sommerfeld track was utilised to form main paths. Each camp had a permanent SOS housekeeping staff of thirty men whose duties were to provide the mess personnel, dig latrines as required, provide fuel for tent stoves, water rations, etc. The SOS personnel occupied five of the living tents. Folding canvas cots were in each living tent and four blankets were issued to each combat soldier. Each assembly area and each camp were identical with the exception that the camps in the assembly areas to process assault troops had complete mess gear while in other assembly areas the transient troops used their own mess kits. The camps were situated immediately adjacent to hedgerows to affect some measure of camouflage and placed to minimise constriction of roads paths etc. For control purposes it was necessary to utilise all space adjacent to hedges excepting those liable to flooding.

The campsites were very muddy. The soil is gummy clay. Sommerfeld matting in the camp areas proved fairly satisfactory.

The tents in each assembly area were set up in a single line adjacent to a two-way road. This provided very little opportunity for camouflage, but the tents blended into the natural background and could not be seen beyond half a mile.

**Troops:** Exercise plans provided for processing of approximately 30,000 troops as far as embarkation points, but actual embarkation was of only 10,242 personnel and 1,096 vehicles in Falmouth area and 260 troops and 21 vehicles in Portsmouth area. To support these troops required 10,000 SOS static service troops, which were required to operate installations and services.

**Service to troops:** Every consideration was given to the well-being of the combat troops during phase 1 of the operation. While quartered in the assembly areas they were relieved of all responsibility for housekeeping in the camps. Best possible meals were served. Two PX and recreation areas were established in each assembly area and prior to leaving the marshalling area candy and cigarettes were issued to each man. It was considered inexpedient for either the driver or relief driver of any vehicle to leave for the meal stop near the hards and therefore arrangements were made to feed these men in their vehicles.

**Medical:** One platoon of the 8th Field Hospital operated 100 of a normally 400-bed hospital. In addition a battalion first aid station was established in a tent at the starting point of each of the assembly areas and at each hard.

**Transit areas:** These contained no shelter but only messing facilities and parking areas and were within ½ mile or 1 mile of embarkation points. Hot meals were provided for all troops arriving at or near meal times. Drivers were fed at their vehicles. 'Topping off' of vehicles was done at this area by drivers using 5-gallon cans brought from assembly areas for this purpose.

**Embarkation Points:** These were 'hards' or piers. Craft carrying only personnel (LCI) were loaded at piers. Craft carrying vehicles or vehicles and personnel (LCTs or LSTs) were loaded at hards which varied in capacity from 2 to 4 craft, either LCT or LST depending on harbour conditions. Hards were of 'chocolate block' construction backed by concrete apron to access road.

**Assault:** Misplacing of craft in waves resulted in confusion. Movement was slow, and Major General Gerow doubted if any of the men landed on one of the beaches would have got off alive. Troops bunched together under simulated fire. Troops were overloaded with equipment and seemed to be road-bound.

**Waterproofing:** Appeared to be adequate but due to dry-shod landings no real test was involved.

**Cranes:** Four cranes were on the beach, two equipped with long booms none of which were being used. They were difficult to manoeuvre in the loose sand beach and therefore not used. In the dump area there were no cranes although two truck mounted cranes were in use.

**Bulldozers:** Plenty of D-7 bulldozers were on hand to carry on all of the required tasks, some units being used to anchor LCTs.

**Recovery tractors:** This valuable piece of equipment was kept very busy, a number being used to anchor LCTs. Owing to steep beach and offshore wind landing craft were broached. A suitable type of land anchor should be provided in order that valuable equipment not be immobilised by being used. Tractors where necessary to assist wheeled vehicles through sand. Vehicle recovery observed consisted mainly in dragging wheeled vehicles up the beach by D-7s and TD-18s until suitable exit roads could be prepared.

**Beach roadway and exits:** Sommerfeld, track chespalling and coir matting were available in large quantities for construction of beach roadways and exits. The coir matting was essential since the loose character of the beach did not permit the use of Sommerfeld track or chespalling alone.

Where the beaches were impassable to all vehicles but tractors, units did not construct turn-arounds at the high water mark but were attempting to operate DUKWs to and from the water and cargo vehicles to and from the beached LCTs over single track roadways with consequent traffic jams. It was necessary to go off the roadway to turn around or else back down a distance of some 100 or 150 yards into craft.

Beach exits gave much trouble due to the nature of the sand. Sommerfeld track gave unsatisfactory results unless laid carefully on smooth sand with matting and chespalling under the track. Eye bars are considered essential to get the most out of this track on soft sand or soft ground. Stakes should be used to hold the eye bar.

Combat engineers in assault constructed a footbridge across a marsh and water area immediately behind the beach. Difficulty was reported due to thick woods. Infantry had worked around flanks of the obstacle before the bridge was finished.

Steel planking and wooden planks were used for turnouts and hard standings and to provide entrances to dumps.

**Camouflage:** Violation of obvious safety precautions occurred from the first. The first assault wave went forward in a compact group despite adjacent hedges providing cover. Signal Corps troops laid wire across open fields. Congestion around a light pontoon bridge was needless, as adjacent gorse would have given good cover. Trench mortars were similarly installed without cover.

Troop formations were held in the centre of the fields. One unit built bivouac fires by night. Supplies discharged between Matthews point were not put under adjacent cover. The 531st Engineers were installed in high woods but gave their positions away by leaving crane carrier trucks in the open. First Engineer Brigade Hq placed pup tents in regular rows on a lawn despite the fact that there was a neighbouring wood.

Trench Mortars were installed in fields without consideration being given to the lessening of visibility, though they could have reached the same targets if placed in the midst of nearby gorse where their obviousness would have been lessened.

Full advantage was not taken of camouflage possibilities, as the efforts in this direction were confined to the siting of tents and similar structures in conformity with natural features.

**Map supply:** Provision was not made for full-scale supply. It is felt that the exercise has been a failure insofar as map supply and distribution is concerned due to the refusal to consider map supply and distribution as though for an actual amphibious operation against an enemy coast.

**Beaching of craft:** The steep beach was a favourable factor with respect to the large tidal variation. However it was found necessary at times to keep a constant strain on a line from a tractor to an LCT on a rising tide to prevent craft from leaving shore. This is a use of tractors which can hardly be permitted on big scale. The need would probably not occur on a flat beach but there appear to be problems in connection with the use of landing craft on beaches during both a rising and a falling tide of large magnitude which should be fully explored if such action has not already been taken.

**Ordnance:** A small advance ammunition depot was operated to issue units any ammunition they might be short of, but their main concern in the exercise was to keep vehicles operating.

Ordnance installations in addition to the ammunition depot included a 500 man tented camp to house personnel, an advanced field depot to issue vehicle parts to units and advanced (medium) field shop for 2nd and 3rd echelon repairs to vehicles, and a vehicle park which contained standard type vehicles for issue to units in cases of serious breakdown. Ordnance also kept trouble-shooting mechanics on patrol in jeeps over the road net of the exercise area. Wreckers were available to extricate any vehicle in difficulty.

**Hospitals**: The 8th Field Hospital was erected by Medical Dept personnel with equipment which included tents, portable generators and medical apparatus. Concrete slabs were used for flooring and were supplemented by pierced steel planking, which was used for paths. Bucket latrines were utilised and water was conveniently stored in Lister bags spaced throughout the hospital area after being drawn from engineer water supply points.

**Traffic**: Some vehicles were landed unloaded; others were overloaded. There was confusion over the inability of the road net to provide for the flow of troops and supplies. Traffic signs were insufficient, and there was poor mud discipline. Vehicles frequently were lined bumper to bumper, and traffic control was poor. A six mile-per-hour convoy speed slowed traffic up too much, and its abolition was advocated. Sufficient beach exits were not opened.

**Communications**: Wire discipline was poor. Signal Corps troops had to set 400 telephone poles and string 250 miles of cable in a very short time, and they did not have the facilities to do a good job. Signal communications in general were hampered by lack of equipment.

**Petrol**: Topping off gasoline tanks at the hards (filling the tanks to the top just before the vehicle was driven on the ship) slowed up loading and was unnecessary. Gasoline supply companies were not equipped with containers to dispense oil and were unable to perform properly. Fire protection for gasoline distribution points and dumps was insufficient.

**Security**: Security was very bad. Camouflage of assembly areas was very poor. Radio silence was consistently violated. A radio intelligence section, without previous knowledge of the situation, obtained a complete battle order of the participating units, the composition of the naval forces, the call signs of the command and alternate command ships, the location of a cannon company platoon, the time Corps headquarters landed, and a list of the ships remaining off the beach overnight.

**Chemical Warfare Service**: A dump was maintained containing portable decontamination apparatus and stocks of chemically impregnated and impermeable clothing.

Some general points we also raised:

- The entire Regimental Combat Team plus all vehicles and artillery were put ashore by dark on the first day. There was considerable delay of the assaulting troops on the beach. In the case of Red beach the troops were forced to remain for a considerable period owing to the delay in being able to cross the marshy ground
- There was a tendency amongst troops on the beach to congregate together rather than maintain wide dispersal
- Assaulting troops in proceeding from the beaches inland did not take full advantage of cover. In a great many instances entire platoons proceeded in virtually squad columns across open fields
- Considerable difficulty was understood to have been encountered in breaking through a pipe scaffolding obstacle using TNT blocks tied to the frame
- In the ammunition depot it was noted that a full strength platoon was standing around watching about eight men unloading ammunition from the DUKW by means of an A-frame
- There did not appear to be enough cargo vehicles to permit continuous unloading of LCTs, which were standing waiting
- Traffic arrangements and provisions on the beach were very poor, particularly with respect to turn-around and routing traffic
- No attempt had been made on the narrow inland roads to knock down fences and earth walls at corners so that the DUKWs could successfully negotiate corners
- Traffic control appeared to be good. Inland routes and MP personnel appeared to be well informed as to the location of various installations
- Effective fire support must be much heavier than that of Exercise Duck

- Assaulting troops must clear the beaches so that troops can stop there. Ways through obstacles must be cleared quickly
- Some beach roadways must be provided before wheeled vehicles can be rapidly cleared from soft beaches.

Despite the detailed critiques, the exercise was thought to have been well planned and smoothly executed although the facilities provided were sufficient to handle many more troops than were involved. The available landing craft were judged to be the limiting factor. The most significant thing observed was the lack of basic training and of organisation and direction in the units. This weakness had been evidenced before during the landings in Sicily and in Italy. Great difficulty was experienced in following loading priorities, and copies of final manifest and stowage plans or hatched lists for unloading failed to arrive. But in spite of these deficiencies, there were many things on the credit side. Exercise Duck went off very smoothly for a first attempt. Loading was particularly good, and it was found that loading time had been greatly overestimated. The marshalling system worked so well that it formed the basis for the 'Neptune' marshalling system. And above all, the assault troops were beginning to master their new amphibious techniques.

Quite rightly the focus of the assault exercises was on the beaches at Slapton Sands. The smaller beach to the north of Slapton Sands however was also utilised. The US Army Engineer observers visited Blackpool Beach on D+1 and their report provides some detail of how this beach was used during the amphibious exercises.

## Blackpool Beach

On the morning of D+1, visitors were permitted to travel by bus to Strete and walk to Blackpool, which had been opened as a maintenance area beach. In passing the assault beaches a single Sommerfeld track roadway led from the water where it was observed that an LCT was discharging vehicles to the highway. No shell holes could be seen as a result of supporting fire, though some of the few shallow foxholes may have originally been shell holes.

At Blackpool, three roadways had been made to the water's edge. They were built of various combinations of Sommerfeld track, chespalling and material resembling burlap but much heavier. Sections of a tubular steel frame obstacle had obviously been dismounted to make way for the exit roads. Two LCTs were apparently being made ready for vehicles to be loaded. This work was proceeding slowly, an attempt being made with a truck in one case and a tractor in the other to pull the craft further ashore (ramps were already practically out of the water), while rolls of roadway material were being piled at the ends of the ramps to improve the approach. The forward end of one LCT was loaded with roadway material, the rear loaded with five-gallon cans; the other was loaded with boxes.

DUKWs apparently were being loaded from craft ashore. Two came in within about five minutes, one carrying a load of large boxes, the other small boxes in cargo nets. The DUKWs moved across the beach by the roadway at the end of which one LCT was stationed. A few minutes later a column of empty trucks started towards the water on the same roadway to let the DUKWs pass. Apparently the beach traffic circulation had not been entirely organised by them (about 0130 D+1).

A layout of the beach dump locations was not seen. A petrol dump for which no stock had arrived was observed in several fields about a mile from the beach. At the beach itself however there was considerable congestion. A number of trucks and DUKWs were closely packed in the open adjacent to the beach roadway, while just across the main road there was a medical clearing station.

## Exercises Duck II and Duck III

Immediately following the critiques of Duck I, plans were begun for exercises Duck II and Duck III. One result of Duck I critiques was the establishment of the planning group on a permanent basis. Its first conference was held on 25 January in the war room of XIX District headquarters, and planning was begun immediately. On 6 February final details were arranged by a planning group staff conference attended by representatives of the 29th Division and the Navy.

It was decided to hold two exercises, Duck II from 7 February, and Duck III from 23 February to 1 March. These two exercises were entirely training exercises, designed to give experience to the other two combat teams of the 29th Infantry Division and to the remaining units of the 1st Engineer Special Brigade which had not participated in Duck I. They were modelled on Duck I, following it in most respects but attempting to avoid its mistakes. Duck II was to include the 116th Regimental Landing Team of the 29th Div, and the 1st Bn of the 531st Engineer Shore Regiment, together with other 1st Brigade elements and attached to V Corps units. Duck III was to include the 115th Regimental Landing Team of the 29th Div and 1st Brigade elements. Small tank and tank destroyer units were to be used for the first time. During the night of 6/7 February, administrative orders for the first exercise were published and on 7 February the movement tables were published. On the same days, casual housekeeping personnel was ordered to report to sector headquarters, and on 9 February, G-3 and G-4 staffs went to the area to coordinate final arrangements between the Navy, the task force and SOS. Movement of the task force personnel into the assembly area began on 9 February with the 1st Brigade personnel moving into Lupton House. The following day, personnel of tanks and tank-destroyer units moved into sub-camps 1, 2 and 3 in camp Z. Other units moved direct from their home stations to the hards. Loading was completed by 2400 hours 12 February. The assault was made 14 February and lasted for two days.

In general, the principal problems encountered were those met in Duck I. They included the difficulties of the navy in placing designated craft at the proper hard, the lack of realisation on the part of the craft commanders that they were responsible for embarkation and for debarkation at the proper points, the lack of road signs, and difficulties in coordination between the services. In most ways the exercise went off more evenly than Duck I. Observation planes reported that camouflage organised by the services was excellent, although concealment of field forces was still bad and would have to be improved in the invasion.

Duck III followed the same general pattern with D-Day taking place on 29 February. The interval between Duck II and Duck III was not sufficient to permit rectification of mistakes in the first exercise. It should be emphasised that the arrangement of units in the three exercises discussed did not follow the Neptune pattern. At the time they were planned, that pattern was not known. Eventually the 29th Div was supported by the 6th Engineer Special

Brigade rather than the 1st Brigade which was placed in support of the 4th Infantry Division.


## Exercise Fox

Exercise Fox was carried out by Force 'O' and involved two RCTs in an assault on the Slapton Sands area. The exercise was ordered by V Corps headquarters on 7 February 1944 and took place over 7–11 March 1944. The assault took place on 11 March 1944 .The troops embarked consisted of part of the V Corps with Major General Gerow, US Army, in command. They were loaded at Weymouth and Portland, the ports which Force 'O' was to use for Operation Neptune. In Operation Fox, APAs (attack transport ships) were used for the first time. The bombarding force consisted of two cruisers and eight destroyers, the latter with additional destroyers and trawlers forming the escorts. As in Exercise Duck, no attempt was made by the Germans to attack the assault forces by sea or air, either during the sea passage or while off the Slapton Sands. On conclusion of the exercise, the APAs were sailed to the Clyde to safeguard them from any possibility of air attacks. Exercise Fox was the largest of the exercises prior to the major rehearsals – Exercises Fabius I and Tiger. The exercise was decided upon by the V Corps Planning Board early in February. It was the only major exercise which paralleled the plans for Neptune, and in a way it constituted a rehearsal for exercise Fabius I, itself the rehearsal for the assault on Omaha Beach.

Detailed planning, however, was held up so that it could parallel planning for Neptune, and little work was done until the publication of First Army's Operation Plan Neptune on 15 February. As a result, planning for Fox was late, and the exercise suffered to some extent. There appears to have been a tendency to regard it as a training exercise rather than as a test of amphibious techniques. The critiques of observers usually begin with such phrases as, 'there were many difficulties and deficiencies which will be cleared up in the next exercise (Fabius I) where there will be more time for adequate planning.'

The marshalling was accomplished by XVIII District and involved entirely new personnel and camps. The whole marshalling plan, however, was worked out according to the doctrine established in the three previous

Duck exercises. The assault pattern was similar to the Neptune plan for the Omaha Beach assault. Units involved were the 16th RCT of the 1st Inf Div and the 116th RCT of the 29th Inf Div, working under control of 1st Inf Div headquarters which, in turn, was under a headquarters group from V Corps. The two combat teams were supported by units of the Provisional Engineer Special Brigade Group. The 37th Eng C Bn of the 5th Eng Sp Brig supported the 16th RCT, and the 149th Eng C Bn of the 6th Eng Sp Brig supported the 116th RCT. Each of the two engineer combat battalions was reinforced with DUKW companies, truck companies, medical and signal detachments, quartermaster troops and port troops to comprise a battalion beach party.

The units began their movement to marshalling areas in Dorset prior to 1 March. There were some difficulties in the marshalling camps because of insufficient time given XVIII District to ready the areas for transient troops, and construction was still going on while the troops were arriving. Embarkation began 7 March and continued through D-Day on 9 March. Plymouth, Weymouth, Dartmouth and Portland were the ports used by the convoy which consisted of 6 APAs, 21 LSTs, 22 LCI(L)s, and 49 LCTs, in addition to LCVPs and salvage craft. Seven quartermaster truck companies were involved, using the normal convoy system on 7 March, and then resorting to a shuttle service for the last two days. A total of 16,923 persons and 1,908 vehicles were processed through the marshalling areas and embarked on the naval craft.

The H-Hour craft assembled and left for the Slapton Sands area the night before D-Day, escorted by five British destroyers and with air cover by the Royal Air Force and the Ninth US Air Force. The assault plan was similar to the Omaha phase of Neptune, with the British landing on the left and the Americans on the right, but the only portion of the plan actually carried out involved the American left flank. The 16th RCT of the 1st Inf Div landed on the right and the 116th RCT of the 29th Inf Div landed on the left, reversing the actual Normandy landings. For the purpose of planning, the 18th RCT of the 1st Div was assumed to land at H+2 hours, and the 26th RCT of the 1st Div on D+1. The 115th RCT was assumed to land on D-Day with the 759th Tk Bn. The two combat teams, which actually landed, came ashore with two battalions abreast and one in reserve. Assault landings were satisfactory, and there was naval gunfire support with live ammunition. Observers agreed however that the build-up and consolidation of the beachhead suffered from hasty planning and preparation. The comparatively green 5th and 6th Engineer Special Brigades fell behind their schedule, and there was considerable confusion among the assault units.

The following weak spots were noted by umpires and special observers:

**Mounting**: Lack of experience on the part of camp personnel was apparent, but camp operation improved as troops gained experience. There was insufficient time to prepare camps, only two and a half days on an average, prior to the reception of transients. Because of the improvement shown, static personnel trained in the exercise were earmarked for future operations. Mess sanitation in the camps was poor, and, on the advice of umpires and observers, cooking schools were organised, kitchens were re-equipped, and new mess sanitation requirements were adopted. The transportation standing operating procedure was found to be too complicated. There were too many forms and too much supervision by military police. Four hours were allocated to loading each LST, but it was found possible to do the job in two hours.

**Assault**: Available critiques fail to give complete details of assault results, but they indicate that the assault suffered from lack of coordination between the Navy and the Army and between various headquarters. This was partially caused by lack of time.

**Security**: Security was spotty. Camouflage was poor, and control within marshalling camps was not good. Telephone warnings of air raids and enemy use of gas was very bad, and measures were taken to move up more comprehensive emergency communications in future exercises and in Neptune.

**Beach Group**: Major criticisms centred around the operations of the beach engineers and the establishment of the beach port. It was found that there were too few loading points for the number of craft involved. There was poor coordination between the beach master and coasters, resulting in the delayed arrival of supplies on the beach. Equipment unloaded from the coasters was in poor condition, and coaster captains had no orders. There was no contact between the Beach Group and naval control headquarters for several hours. Beach communications were poor, and there was no communication between beach headquarters and the dumps until D+1. Wire teams laid their lines during the night because of the delay in bringing equipment ashore. Twenty DUKWs had been allocated to each coaster for unloading, and it was found that ten were sufficient to do the job. Later waves of troops came ashore in the wrong order, creating confusion. For example, medical clearing personnel came in at H+2 hours, but could do no work until their equipment arrived at H+11 hours.

There were bright spots as well. For example, fifteen DUKWs were brought ashore preloaded with balanced loads of ammunition for emergency issue, and this proved so satisfactory that it was incorporated in plan Neptune. Waterproofing was carried further than in any previous exercise, and all vehicles were waterproofed and then de-waterproofed after landing. New methods and compounds were used and proved satisfactory.

## Exercise Beaver

In exercise Beaver (29–31 March) the 8th and 22nd RCTs of the 4th Division, reinforced by a 1st Eng Sp Brig detachment, two companies of the 1106th Eng Gp, the 502nd Parachute Infantry Regiment, and the Ninth Air Force (Major General Barton) and attached units, were loaded and sailed from Plymouth, Dartmouth, and Brixham, in LSTs and LCI(L)s. In order to make a good approach to the Slapton beach, the assault forces took a circular route around the western half of Lyme Bay. Bombardment was carried out by two cruisers and four destroyers while all other available ships were used as escorts and covering forces. Two minesweeping flotillas swept ahead of the assault forces.

This operation again followed the plan and facilities as used in the Duck exercises. Marshalling and embarkation areas were located in the Brixham-Plymouth district, and Slapton Sands was used as the assault area. Group 2 of the 11th Amphibious Force provided the lift, protected the assault convoy and supported the landing. The previous exercises had been ordered by VII Corps headquarters but had been almost entirely carried out by the 4th Division. Beaver however found the VII Corps an active participant. Disembarkation and the beach assault went according to plan. The assault units secured a bridgehead and made a rapid advance inland. Following the D-Day advance, the units were re-supplied and reorganised for extended operations. About 1,800 tons of supplies were unloaded from two coasters, and as a part of the exercise, the combat units were re-supplied with ammunition on the night of D-Day. Exercise Beaver was considered a disappointment to many who participated. A certain amount of confusion existed and some units failed to perform their respective missions.

One account states that it was 'far from successful mainly for its confusion: coordination broke down between units and the men who took part.'[2]

## Exercise Trousers

The 3rd Canadian Infantry Division who formed Force 'J' and who would assault Juno Beach on D-Day itself performed this exercise. It was planned to exercise the naval assault force in the passage, approach and assault landing, and also to exercise signal communications and fire support in the assault. The exercise took place on 12 April 1944. The 2nd Canadian Corps had 4 Special Service Brigade (less three commandos) under its command and was to assault between Dartmouth and Newton Ferrers and to advance to and secure by last light D-Day a covering position along the general line Totnes-Brixton.

The assault would comprise two brigades assaulting the right flank and one (simulated) brigade of the 1st Canadian Infantry Division assaulting the left flank.

A special force known as Bing Force, composed of armoured cars and special RE troops was also to land on 3 Canadian Infantry Division beaches. This force was to push forward as soon as coastal defences had been overcome and to destroy the bridge over the River Avon. This force was to impose maximum delay on the enemy and withdraw on orders of the Force Commander. The assault beaches were codenamed 'Able' and 'Baker' sectors. The 8 Canadian Infantry Brigade Group would land on the Baker sector and the 7 Canadian Infantry Brigade Group on the Able sector. The reserve brigade was the 9 Canadian Brigade Group. Landings would end at the first tide and conclude on capture of divisional intermediate objective. Loading would take place at Southampton.

The exercise was to be performed in two phases:

Phase I      Capture of the beachhead
Phase II     Capture of divisional intermediate objective

After establishing a beachhead the plan was to advance to a pre-determined safety line. Troops and vehicles were not to go beyond this line until after H+120. Firing restrictions imposed by Slapton range orders caused this. The naval component comprised four HQ ships: HMS *Hilary:* HQ, transporting 3 Canadian Infantry Division; HMS *Lawford*, transporting 7 Canadian Infantry Brigade; HMS *Waveney*, transporting 8 Canadian Infantry Brigade; and the SS *Isle of Thanet*, transporting 9 Canadian Infantry Brigade. The landing craft component comprised 9 LSTS, 20 LSIs, 110 LCTs, and 12 LCIs. Additionally 2 Cruisers, 4 destroyers and sundry miscellaneous craft would also take part.

## Exercise Trousers – Detail of Events

| H–60 | DDs proceed in shore |
| H–40 | Destroyers bombardment opens |
| H–30 | SP artillery opens fire |
| H–25/15 | Air attacks on field artillery positions |
| H–20 | Flank protection by LCGs commences |
| H–15 | LCT(A) HE open fire on beach defences, LCT(R) fire |
| H–5 | DDs touch down and open fire. Ground strafing by air |
| H–2 | LCA(HR) fire |
| H–Hour | AVRE and LCT(A) touch down |
| H+5 | Assault Companies landing. LCT(A)HE firing by FOOs |
| H+15 | Locality attacked and captured (262673) |
| H+20 | Locality captured (251655) |
| H+20 | Reserve company and Bn HQ landing |
| H+ 30 | ABSS established |
| H+ 35 | Destroyers fire on call of FOBs |

| | |
|---|---|
| H+ 35/40 | Guns captured (236683) |
| H+40 | Guns captured (244686) |
| H+45 | MBSO established |
| H+50 | BSS established Able and Baker Beaches |
| H+60 | Beachhead secured |
| H+60 | Bing Force landing |
| H+ 60/75 | First priority vehicles landing |
| H+ 85 | Widdicombe Ho & Beeson mopped up |
| H+90 | SP artillery landing |
| H+90 | Bing Force moves off |
| H+125 | Forward troops at report line 'Snake' |
| H+130 | Sp artillery preparing to open on land |
| H+140 | Remainder assault brigades land |
| H+150/210 | Order Reserve brigade to land |
| H+200/230 | Divisional intermediate objective captured. |

In all approximately 5,000 Personnel and 870 vehicles were involved in this exercise.

## Exercise Tiger

The purpose of Exercise Tiger was to conduct a rehearsal of Force 'U', Operation Overlord in which actual plans, formations and conditions were adhered to as closely as limitations of equipment and facilities would permit. It would be the last exercise in which Force 'U' participated before D-Day itself. All British, Canadian and American units scheduled to assault the Caen-Isigny area were to participate in the Fabius exercises which were broken into separate sections, four British and four American. The Utah beachhead, being considered to some extent a separate operation, called for a separate rehearsal. Exercise Tiger was held under the direction of VII Corps.

Tentative high-level planning for Tiger began early in February, but definite instructions were not issued until 1 April. Though conforming in principle to the previous Exercise Beaver, it was on a larger scale and was carried on, as far as possible, with those landing craft to be used in the actual operation.

The route of the assault force was taken well into the middle of Lyme Bay, so as to give a longer sea passage. The actual approach was marked by lighted dan buoys laid by the minesweeping units. Two cruisers and seven destroyers carried out both direct and indirect bombardment from H-50 to H-Hour. As in the other exercises, the maximum number of destroyers, corvettes and trawlers available formed the escort group and covering force. Emphasis was placed on the establishment and maintenance of communication between all supported and supporting forces. Camouflage discipline was stressed in the concentration area and during the exercise. Taking part in the exercise were 25,000 men and 2,750 vehicles. The exercise would take place over the period 26–30 April. The plan was to process all of the participating troops through the concentration and marshalling areas and to embark the proper scales of equipment that would be used on D-Day. Movement overseas was under the control of the US Navy and a pre-arranged naval fire support plan and air support plan would take place prior to the actual assault landing. The planned assault on Utah Beach included extensive airborne operations by the 101st and 82nd Airborne divisions. Because the aircraft necessary to duplicate the D-Day operation were not available, and due to the restrictions on dropping airborne troops imposed by the Slapton Sands training area, the employment of these two divisions was to be on a limited scale. Four hours before H-Hour troops of the 101st Airborne Division were to arrive in the Slapton Sands area by vehicle and simulate an airborne landing. They were to arrive east of Kingsbridge and seize the high ground west of the beach. Three airborne naval shore fire control parties would also be attached to the 101st Airborne Division, and nine naval shore fire control parties operating from 286th joint assault signal company would operate with the 4th Infantry Division. Three air support parties from the 9th Air Force would also participate. The 82nd Airborne Division were to perform a simulated landing at dawn on D+1 west of Ermington to prevent enemy reinforcements advancing towards the bridgehead.

The exercise was broken down into four phases. Phase 1 (26 April) consisted of the movement to concentration areas, processing through concentration and marshalling areas and embarkation. Phase II (27 April) consisted of movement by sea, debarkation, and assault of the beach defences up to the establishment of the initial beach defence line. Phase III

(28 April) consisted of the consolidation and extension of the beachhead, concentration of forces involved in preparation for return movement to home stations or marshalling areas. Phase IV (29 April) was the final phase and would exercise the completion of unloading and continuation of operation of beach maintenance areas.

Concentration took place in Dartmouth and eastern Plymouth areas. Embarkation was to take place from Dartmouth, Brixham, Torquay, and Plymouth. Service ammunition was to be fired and fire support rendered by air and naval units that would approximate the plans for Overlord as closely as possible, as the availability of craft, weather and ammunition would permit.

All three regimental landing teams of the 4th Infantry Division took part. These were to be concentrated in areas around Plymouth and East Dartmouth. Two were to be loaded from the Dartmouth-Brixham-Torquay area and one from Plymouth. The 1st Engineer Special Brigade was to be in direct support, and mounting was to be undertaken by XIX District following the Duck-Beaver formula, but with measures taken to correct errors and deficiencies shown up by these exercises.

The 11th Amphibious Force was to provide the lift. A medical plan included the handling of simulated casualties. These casualties were designated by umpires who affixed tags designating the type of injury. They were required to be returned through the casualty evacuation process as real casualties to the beach battalion medical services where they would be dispersed to ships.

In all, 25,000 men and 2,750 vehicles were to be embarked. The landing beaches were centred on the Slapton Sands beach and designated Uncle Red (western landing beach) and Tare Green (eastern landing beach). The exercise lasted nine days, with six given over to mounting and embarkation. Troops entered the marshalling areas beginning 22 April, and D-Day was 28 April.

There was considerable delay in distributing plans and orders, and the result was a certain amount of improvisation, although the marshalling camps were not greatly affected. However loading tables, in some cases, had to be rewritten during the exercise, and many of the naval craft arrived at their hards very late. This resulted in traffic jams and confusion. The actual landings were favoured by good weather, and the exercise proceeded according to plan. Assault troops went ashore after a pre-H-Hour naval bombardment of the simulated enemy defences, which reduced the pillboxes, cut through wire entanglements. The troops then made their way inland to join the elements of the 101st Airborne Division which had arrived previously deployed. At the same time elements of the 1st Engineer Special Brigade went ashore, swept minefields, opened up beach exits, laid tracked roads, and established dumps.

Unloading activities began on D-Day and were closely watched by representatives of Service of Supply and First Army. The latter headquarters had ordered a total of 2,200 tons of supplies unloaded in the first two days. On the first tide on D-Day, two LCTs each with 200 tons of supplies were unloaded over the high water mark; on the second tide, two coasters with 1,500 tons of supplies were unloaded; and on D+1, six LBVs preloaded with 50 tons of supplies each were unloaded.

A witness to the exercise was Captain Harry Butcher, a naval aide to the supreme commander, General Dwight Eisenhower. Captain Butcher watched the exercises from a landing craft:

*H-Hour was to have been at 7:30 a.m. unless the weather was so bad the aircraft could not participate, in which event it was to have been at 7 o'clock. As the naval bombardment started on schedule and the weather seemed perfect, with a smooth sea, we assumed H-Hour was 7:30 as advertised. The LCTs bearing waterproofed, tanks called DDs were in position to be launched at 7:15.*

*Then there was a delay in the landing; why, we did not know, although later we heard that H-Hour had been postponed even after the naval bombardment had begun for one hour. Then the first assault wave of infantry in LCVPs arrived from the transport vessels eight miles out. They landed either with or shortly after the amphibious tanks. This landing was preceded by rocket bombardment, at the postponed H-Hour, from three landing craft that had crept close to shore and fired diagonally at the obstacles, including barbed wire, tank ditch, and other prepared positions. The rockets had made usable pathways through the barbed wire.*

*In this exercise, effort was made to get tanks ashore quickly in order to use their fire power. Engineers were brought in as rapidly as possible to demolish obstacles with hand-placed explosives. The tanks had to wait while these operations proceeded. If there had been enemy fire, the tanks, being quite close together, would have been easy targets, as, indeed, would the landing craft.*[3]

The unfortunate sinking of the LSTs en-route to the exercise by German torpedo boats greatly marred the build-up and supply phases of the exercise, reducing the beach party practically to its assault phase elements. Critiques of the mounting and assault indicate that results otherwise were fairly satisfactory, although there was a tendency on the part of officers and men to treat Tiger as another problem in a long series. By this time exercises had become routine, particularly for the 1st Brigade, which had taken part in fifteen exercises from January through April. Observers reported that many officers were inclined to dismiss shortcomings as unimportant, and to feel that when the invasion took place, deficiencies shown in Tiger and other exercises would no longer exist. Mounting, in particular, showed great improvement, particularly in regard to the operation of the camps. There were a few flaws, such as lack of sufficient briefing tents, and the fact that a large shipment of jerrycans had just arrived with each can painted yellow so that it was easily seen from the air. Security in the camps was improved, although a lack of uniformity in the pass system was criticised. Camouflage was better than in previous exercises, and signal installations were found to be adequate.

During the period 1–18 May, units which had lost heavily in personnel and equipment during Tiger and the E-boat attack were re-equipped and replacements were secured. The 3206th Quartermaster Service Company, which had been practically wiped out, was replaced by the 363rd Quartermaster Service Company, and the 557th Quartermaster Railhead Company, which had lost very heavily, was replaced by the 562nd Quartermaster Railhead Company.

Captain Harry Butcher in his account of Exercise Tiger concluded:

*I came away from the exercise feeling depressed. But frequently the poorest kind of exercise presages the best actual operation because the failures are noticed and corrected. Later that evening when I joined the General's train at Taunton, I heard Ike, Bradley, Gerow, and Tedder in an earnest discussion of today's problem. They asked me if I had heard the reason for the postponement of H–Hour. I replied I had not and was surprised that they did not know either. Gerow emphasized the principle: never change the time once it is set, because too much confusion arises.*[4]

## Exercise Fabius

This was the last major amphibious exercise before Operation Overlord.

The six Fabius exercises together constituted the greatest amphibious exercise in history, and immediately followed Exercise Tiger. While Tiger concerned only Force 'U', the units that were to assault Utah Beach, Fabius included all of the other four invasion assault forces and the two major build-up forces which were to invade France.

Fabius was made up of six separate exercises as follows:

**Fabius I** was the rehearsal for Assault Force 'O', those elements of the 1st US Infantry Division, the 29th US Infantry Division, the Provisional Engineer Special Brigade Group, and attached units, which were to assault Omaha Beach under the command of V Corps. This force marshalled in area D, embarked from the Portland–Weymouth area, and landed at Slapton Sands.

**Fabius II** was the rehearsal for Assault Force 'G', elements of the British 50th Infantry Division and attached units, which were to assault Gold Beach. This force marshalled in areas C and B, embarked from Southampton and Lymington, and landed on Hayling Island.

**Fabius III** was the rehearsal for Assault Force 'J', elements of the Canadian 3 Infantry Division and attached units which were to assault Juno Beach. This force marshalled in areas A and C, embarked from Southampton and Gosport, and landed at Bracklesham Bay.

**Fabius IV** was the rehearsal for Assault Force 'S', elements of the British 3rd Infantry Division and attached units which were to assault Sword Beach. This force marshalled in area A and in the British Southeast Command area, embarked from Gosport and Portsmouth, and landed near Littlehampton.

**Fabius V** was a marshalling exercise for British units in the initial build-up of forces for Gold, Juno and Sword beaches. It concerned that part of the force leaving from the Thames estuary and from east coast ports.

**Fabius VI** was a marshalling exercise for Force 'B', together with British units leaving from southern ports. The American build-up force used about half of marshalling area D and the ports of Portland and Weymouth. The

British build-up force used about half of marshalling area C and the port of Southampton.

Fabius I, II, III and IV were carried out simultaneously under the direction of 21st Army Group. They began on 23 April and ended 7 May. During the period 23–26 April, residues were detached and briefing was carried out. Marshalling began 27 April and craft were loaded 29 April and 1 May. D-Day was originally scheduled for 2 May, but was postponed one day after the marshalling began. Fabius V and VI were scheduled to be held 4–6 May, but due to the postponement of the other exercises, did not actually end until 7 May. Coordination between the six exercises was on a high level, and planning for them was carried on separately by the various commands concerned. The following account concerns only the American exercise, Fabius I.

Fabius, like Tiger, had little of the experiment in its make-up. D-Day was only a month away, and most units participating in the exercise were to return not to their home stations, but to the marshalling areas, there to await the actual invasion. No longer was there time for drastic revisions in plan or for retraining units. Minor deficiencies could be corrected, but Fabius was primarily an exercise to give the troops experience in their tasks and to give the invasion machinery a chance to function as a whole before it would be called upon to perform its primary invasion. Every effort was made to duplicate the conditions to be met on the Normandy beaches, and planning orders called for the exercise to resemble Neptune as closely as limitations of equipment and facilities would permit. Approximately 25,000 troops were processed through the marshalling areas, embarked, and landed on Slapton Sands. After the exercise had completed, they returned to the marshalling areas to await D-Day.

Units participating included the 16th and 18th regimental landing teams of the 1st Infantry Division, the 116th Regimental Combat Team of the 29th Infantry Division, the 347th and 348th Engineer Construction battalions of the 5th Engineer Special Brigade, the 149th Engineer Construction Battalion of the 6th Engineer Special Brigade, the 741st and 743rd Tank battalions, the 2nd and 5th Ranger battalions, and other units attached either to the infantry divisions or to the Provisional Engineer Special Brigade Group.

The overall plan was drafted by First Army headquarters, but the more detailed planning began with V Corps and continued through the various units to battalion level. The tactical plan followed Neptune closely. After a preliminary air and naval bombardment (the former simulated) two battalions of DD tanks were to land at H-Hour, followed by the first wave of infantry. Landing Team 16 was to land on the left and Landing Team 116 on the right. Engineers were to follow immediately, blow underwater obstacles, open up beach exits, and de-mine suspected areas. At H+3 hours, landing team 18 was to land and join the other teams in an attack inland. Three Ranger companies were to land at Blackpool Beach approximately two miles north of Slapton Sands to destroy enemy artillery installations, precisely as Rangers were to land at Pointe du Hoc in Normandy. Another company was to land on the right flank of the regular assault beach, while other Rangers were to be landed with the infantry and were to make their way to the right to relieve the flanking company. Additional troops were to pour ashore, establish the beach, unload cargo, establish dumps, and set up supply installations.

In general, the movement was smooth and operation of the camps encountered no outstanding difficulties. Embarkation also went according to plan with the two 1st Division combat teams loading at Weymouth and Poole, and the 116th landing team loading at Portland. There were 168 craft in the convoy in addition to support vessels. Included were 100 LCTs, 8 LCT(A)s, 21 LCI(L)s, 23 LST(S)s, 3 LSI(H)s, 2 LSI(L)s, 3 XAPs, 4 APAs, and 1 LSH. With most of the craft loaded, D-Day for all Fabius exercises was postponed for twenty-four hours by 21 Army Group because of unfavourable weather.

The assault was launched on schedule. The convoy approached behind minesweepers and marshalled about ten miles offshore. Two cruisers, HMS *Glasgow* and USS *Augusta* were to bombard targets in the assault area between H-40 and H-Hour. The Headquarter Ship was the USS *Ancon*. Swimming DD tanks of the 741st and 743rd Tk Bn were launched 3,000 yards from shore and assaulted the beach at H-Hour. These tanks did not leave the water's edge in the exercise. After the preliminary phase, they proceeded under their own power to Torcross and withdrew from the assault. Normal tanks which were loaded on LCT(A)s were so placed as to be able to fire when the craft were approaching the beach. Later, they were landed by normal means. As the 16th and 116th Regimental Combat teams made their way inland, the 18th Regimental Combat Team was landed together with engineer troops. Four beaches were opened, and their designations were the same as the designations of the Normandy beaches. The 37th Battalion Beach Group landed on Easy Red Beach, opened two beach exit roads; the 149th Battalion Beach Group, landing on Easy Green and Dog Red Beaches, opened two beach exits; and the 348th Battalion Beach Group, landing on Fox Green Beach, took over the operation of one beach exit. Some engineer units, including the headquarters of the 5th and 6th brigades and the Engineer Special Brigade Group, took part in the exercise but did not make the sea voyage. They moved by motor to Slapton Sands and set up their installations after the initial assault. Token supplies were landed by the engineers. On the first tide two LCTs, each loaded with 200 tons of emergency supplies, were unloaded over the high water mark, and on the second tide, 1500 tons of supplies were unloaded by DUKWs and LCTs from coasters. On D+1, six LBVs, each with 50 tons of supplies, were unloaded. The supplies included considerable engineering equipment such as treadway bridging, Sommerfeld track, coir matting and chespalling, which was used to build and improve beach roads.

Fabius I showed up additional flaws in operations, and wherever possible these were corrected before the invasion, although time was running out. Deficiencies in the operations of the beach engineers, emphasised in the critiques, included the following:

**Traffic and Personnel**: Personnel embarkation rosters were not picked up from incoming ships, and their form reports of personnel passed across the beaches were not received. Military police were not loaded in time to control traffic, and there were not enough military police for all-important posts. Signs to direct traffic were not available early enough, and military police had not been sufficiently briefed on the operation. Vehicles were allowed to bunch on the beach while awaiting their assignments, thus presenting profitable targets for enemy artillery and planes.

**Supplies**: Unloading tallies were not maintained and consequently accurate situation reports could not be maintained. DUKWs generally were loaded too light, loads averaging about two tons. (While this was the rated capacity of the amphibians, trials had shown that they were capable of carrying up to five tons without difficulty). There were too many DUKWs for the number of coasters, and unloading of coasters was delayed because of failure to return cargo nets from the beach.

**Signal**: Telephone lines were put of commission much of the time due to lack of care in laying wire. Signal personnel were not landed in time to perform their job. The communications section of one company did not come ashore until after the company had been operational for several hours.

**Medical**: Clearing station personnel of both brigades and the 5th Brigade's clearing station equipment were late in arriving, hampering both treatment and evacuation.

**Dump Operations**: Signs were posted very late, and there was little uniformity. Trucks thus had difficulty in locating the dumps. Dump reports generally were very poor.

While every attempt was made to rectify these conditions prior to the invasion, the difficulty of so doing in the brief time available is shown by the fact that most of the criticisms later were applied to operations during the initial phase of Neptune. As the units completed their move to the hards and began the trip to their home stations, the units from Fabius I returned from the assault area and re-entered the camps, to remain there until called upon to embark for the invasion of France.

This exercise included a significant element of air support. It was provided by aircraft from the Second Tactical Air Force and the US IX Air Force. Prior to the exercise all formation leaders and pilots had familiarised themselves with the assault area at Slapton Sands by overflying the location. Instructions were issued that formations would not fly below 4,000 feet over convoys, and over the assault beach areas fighter-bombers were not to fly below 3,000 feet. In rear areas (over landing strip and gun positions) fighter-bombers could fly as low as 1,500 feet if it was deemed necessary for the completion of their mission.

The air-to-ground beach targets were to be marked with parallel white lines, one at each end of the target. Streets of simulated towns to be attacked were marked with white lime.

Bombing was restricted to targets in the 'units shore impact area' and there was to be no live bombing or firing after H-Hour. The actual boundaries of the range were marked on the ground by white posts.

Marauder aircraft carried out live bombing with rocket-firing Typhoons executing simulated rocket and cannon attacks (no rockets were to be carried on the aircraft).

Attacks were made from east to west. Pyrotechnic signals would be used to indicate cease-firing in case of emergency (1 red star cluster, 1 green star cluster, 1 white star cluster). Actual enemy action and end of exercise would also be indicated using flares. All formations were required to fire the colour of the day so that naval vessels and the assault forces could positively identify them.

Schedule of air activity For Fabius 1:

| Time of Attack | Description of Target | British | American | Type of Aircraft |
|---|---|---|---|---|
| H-30 to H-20 | Beach Defences | | Detailed by IX AF | 9 Marauders |
| H-30 to H-20 | Beach Defences | | ' | ' |
| H-20 to H-15 | Town (imaginary) | | ' | ' |
| H-20 to H-15 | Town (imaginary) | | ' | ' |
| H-20 to H-15 | Town (imaginary) | | ' | ' |
| H-10 to H-5 | Battery position | 182 Squadron | | 12 rocket-firing Typhoons |
| H-10 to H-5 | Battery position | 247 Squadron | | 12 rocket-firing Typhoons |
| H-10 to H-5 | Battery position | 175 Squadron | | 12 rocket-firing Typhoons |
| H-Hour to H-10 | Landing strip | | 358 Group | 1 Group P47's |
| H-Hour to H-20 | Opportunity targets | | 362 Group | 1 Squadron P47's |

## Other Assault Exercises

As well as the major exercises, a number of small and medium sized exercises were also carried out. Force 'U' commenced intensive training with two medium sized exercises, Muskrat (24–27 March) and Beaver (29–31 March).

Muskrat I, carried out in the Clyde, consisted of ship-to-shore training from APA of the 12th Regimental Combat Team of the 4th Division, US Army. The APAs then sailed to the Slapton area. Muskrat II concluded this exercise with a landing and assault on the beach. Two cruisers bombarded, and escorts were provided by destroyers, corvettes, and trawlers. Rear-Admiral Moon sailed with the Assault Forces in his flagship, USS *Bayfield*, a converted APA, but as a spectator only. Captain Maynard, USN, commanding the APAs of Force 'U', was the Task Force Commander. The difficulties in planning with which Force 'U' had to contend were illustrated by the fact that the operation orders of Muskrat II were written by officers lent from Force 'O' without consultation with the Task Force Commander, who was then witnessing Muskrat I, and so out of telephonic communication. These same officers, assigned to Admiral Moon's staff, were working night and day preparing for exercise Beaver, which was to take place shortly.

## Muskrat I

This exercise was held on 13–23 March by the 12th Infantry Regiment, which embarked at Plymouth on three APAs (transports) which moved to the Firth of Clyde in Scotland. There the regimental combat team participated in battalion landing team exercises.

## Muskrat II

Held on 24–26 March by the 12th Infantry Regiment, reinforced by a 1st Engineer Special Brigade detachment, this was really a continuation of Muskrat I, and extended the landing exercises in Scotland at the battalion team level.

## Otter I

This exercise was held on 15–18 March by the 3rd Battalion of the 8th Regimental Combat Team, reinforced. It consisted of a day of instruction and two daylight assault landings in the Slapton Sands area. The exercise mounted from Dartmouth.

## Otter II

Based on the same plan as Otter I, this exercise was held on 19–22 March by the 1st Battalion of the 8th Regimental Combat Team. The 2nd Battalion had been designated the reserve battalion for Neptune and did not engage in a separate exercise.

## Mink I

Held on 15–18 March at Slapton Sands by the 1st Battalion of the 22nd Regimental Combat Team, this exercise followed the same plan as that used in the Otter exercises.

## Mink II

Held on 19–22 March by the 2nd Battalion of the 22nd Regimental Combat Team, this exercise also followed the Otter plan. The 3rd Battalion of the 22nd Regimental Combat Team was to be in reserve for Neptune and no exercise was held for it.

## Cargo V

Held on 1–11 April a Slapton Sands, the 6th Engineer Special Brigade performed duties in support of a task force (assumed) to develop beach and dump facilities including road construction.

As the last of the amphibious exercises ended, all that could be done had been done. The next operation would be the real thing. Thousands of men were primed to perform the greatest amphibious operation of all time. The wheel would spin, the die was cast. When it came to rest, it would read life or death for some men. Victory or defeat, the value of all the training and preparation, would be put to the test.

*Chapter Eleven*

# In Their Own Words: First-hand Accounts from Those who Took Part

For the men that took part in the exercises at Slapton Sands, this was only a short part of a long journey. Official records of training exercises are often sparse and the memory of soldiers taking part in exercises is often ephemeral.

In peacetime, training might provide a break from the boredom of barrack life, but in wartime it has an extra edge – there will soon be real fighting, and real lives will be at stake. The following recollections help give a fresh insight into the assault training exercises at Slapton Sands. They are from a cross section of those who participated: from those who would be performing the assault as well as from those in specialist units that would land after the initial assault phase was complete.

Many of the men taking part in the actual assault had not taken part in combat before. The men of the 4th Infantry Division who would form 'Force U' and assault Utah Beach had arrived directly from the US and were based in the South Devon area. They had never seen combat before. Likewise, the 101st Airborne division that made up part of the massive American airborne assault had also arrived directly from the US. On the other hand, the elements of the 90th Infantry Division that formed part of 'Force U', the men of 82nd Airborne – part of the airborne assault and the 1st Infantry Division forming 'Force O' and landing at Omaha Beach – they had all been in combat in the Mediterranean theatre.

Second Lieutenant John Good, Royal Marines, an officer under training, was sent to Thurlstone. Much of the work there was classroom based, but during the practice assault landings at Slapton, his course was allowed to witness the dress rehearsal by one of the American assault divisions preparing for France:

*I've yet to meet another British serviceman who had our luck. How on earth we were allowed I don't know, but our Course Officer – an excellent chap, Major Jerram – somehow managed it.*

*And so we found ourselves standing on some high ground at the south end of Slapton Sands watching this invasion practice. It was absolutely amazing. I remember so clearly; all our diagrams, learned in the classroom, becoming reality. You looked down onto the bay, and there it all was, in front of your very eyes. Including the fire support – guns, rockets, the full works. And as it progressed we were able to watch the big LSTs coming in and beaching. I think I learned more from those few hours about amphibious operation than any amount of classroom work could ever have taught me.[1]*

During some of the exercises, men of the Airborne Division took part. Not performing actual jumps they were deployed by vehicle. Private William J. Stone, Battery B, 321st Glider Field Artillery, on detached service with the 506 PIR as an artillery forward observer, recalls his experiences of deploying on exercise at Slapton Sands:

*The airborne activity was simulated. Parachute elements were formed up onto sticks just as we would be if we were loaded into C-47s. At about 3am the sticks began walking across the simulated drop zone area. Every 50ft or so the last man in the stick would drop off. This continued until all sticks had jumped . Upon a signal we assembled and moved out on our missions. Glider elements, including the 321st, started their simulated landings at about 6.30am and then moved into position. During the exercise the 321st fired their howitzers in support of the 506th, but did not use live ammunition. The firing was just straight service practice.[2]*

Private David Kenyon Webster of Easy Company, 506 PIR, recalls seeing the assault fleet whilst deployed on Exercise Tiger on 26 April 1944:

*We could see a vast fleet of amphibious craft moving slowly in to land. I've never seen so many ships together at one time; an invasion fleet is the most impressive sight in the world.[3]*

Private James 'Slim' McCann, Company H, 2nd Battalion, 506 PIR, describes how the casualty evacuation process was tested:

*We marched up the hill near a British AA (anti-aircraft) gun position and were told to dig in. We could see the amphibious forces practicing storming the beach below. We had been issued with every item of equipment that we would be expected to carry with us into Normandy on June 6, including three days worth of K-rations. Even the medical battalion received realistic training. They came up the hill stopping at about every fifth foxhole informing the occupant that he was designated 'wounded'. The soldier was than treated and tagged with a label stating 'leg wounded' or some other injury. The stretcher-bearers then carried them off down the hill onto landing craft, where they were transported out to the hospital ship and 'treated'. I was glad I wasn't tagged because I had a chronic seasickness problem.[4]*

The amphibious training was tough for those taking part.

Sergeant John R. Slaughter, D Company, 1st Battalion, 116th Infantry:

*Amphibious training began in earnest when the regiment moved to tented camps in Hampshire. The training area was selected because it resembled the terrain and beaches of Normandy. Slapton Sands near Dartmouth was a sloping expanse of sand and shingle guarded by an arm-pit deep salt marsh which had to be crossed before assaulting simulated fortified bunkers.*

*One of the men in my squad, Pfc Joseph Alvalio, from Brooklyn, was only recently drafted and hadn't fully embraced the system. When he crossed the lake he lost a $6 machine-gun water can in the murky water. On hearing of this mishap, Captain Schilling, the company commander screamed at me: 'Slaughter, what in the hell's the matter with your squad! Bust him to private! He pays for the water can and he's going to learn to take care of his equipment.*

*The company hiked all day dripping wet on the cold and windy moors and slept that night in all the same damp clothes. It was one of the most miserable experiences I can remember as a soldier[5].*

Staff Sergeant Harley A. Reynolds, Company B, 16th Infantry Regiment:

*At Slapton Sands we would make practice landings. We would unload in landing craft and make everything as realistic as possible. We carried live ammo on the last landing and were allowed to fire at make-believe targets on the hills in front of us. We fired at rocks, clumps of shrubbery, dark spots, and white chalk spots, and when rabbits suddenly came out of their burrows they gave us moving targets.*[6]

Thomas Lester, Company M, 116th Infantry Regiment:

*The 29th Division had been in England over a year and they were physically in great shape. We were shown no mercy. I thought they were going to kill me at first but soon got used to the seven day a week training. We went on a twenty-five mile hike every week. This hike was really tough until us replacements got in shape. We trained some on the moors and it seemed to rain all the time. As June 6th got closer we did dry runs with the Navy. We would load on the ships and go out into the ocean and load on to LCVPs and make a landing. We trained at Slapton Sands more than anywhere else when it came to landings. We were well trained by D-Day.*[7]

Second Lieutenant Richard J. Ford, Company K, 115th Infantry Regiment:

*We had a large practice landing at a place called Slapton Sands. This was on a battalion scale. The local people had been evacuated from this area to depth of five to ten miles from shore. We made landings and blew up wire defences with Bangalore torpedoes (4ft length of 2 inch pipe filled with TNT). These lengths were coupled by lugs. We put a block of gun cotton at the connections so they would detonate as a single piece. You coupled the lengths and slid them through the barbed wire. When they exploded it blew a hole about 4 feet wide in the wire. The locals had left signs on their house to not damage them. At the end of the mile limit, field kitchens had been set up to feed the men. You had been on the water for about four days and this was your first hot meal. The kitchen had to be ready to serve hot food to any number of men that came along. You didn't know how many would show up. I was in charge of one of these kitchens, manned by men from 110th Field Artillery.*[8]

Second Lieutenant William C. Frodsham Jr, Company G, 175th Infantry Regiment:

*In late December 1943 we started the first of a series of full scale amphibious exercises preparing for the invasion. The British civilians in the area of Slapton Sands on the coast near Dartmouth, Devon, site of the Royal Naval Academy, had been evacuated from their homes so that the beach could be used by the Americans as a final rehearsal area for the D-Day operation. Slapton Sands was an ideal beach for practice. High ground backed up most of the beach and the tides were nearly the same as those of Normandy.* [9]

As with all military exercises, the experience will vary depending on how individuals are involved. Inevitably some troops taking part had a less taxing experience than others.

Pvt. Howard G. DeVoe, Defence Platoon, HQ Company, 3rd Battalion, 531st Engineer Shore Regiment, 1st Engineer Special Service Brigade:

*During Operation Tiger, I was sitting out there with half a dozen guys for three days having a good time smoking, eating K rations, shooting the breeze. Our situation was to provide the defence. We just stayed there for three days and no one came around except our platoon sergeant. Just six guys sitting out there a mile and a half on the south flank of Slapton Sands. We saw a plane bombing Plymouth, the searchlights go on and they got him. This plane crash happened a couple of miles away from us; the pilot was the only one killed or injured. He bailed out, landed within a half mile of us, and he was picked up by some men of our unit.* [10]

The training for the combat troops involved in the assault on the beach could be extremely tough. They would be the ones to spearhead the attack on Hitler's fortress Europe. To successfully achieve the landings, many different types of skill would be called on. The men involved in these technical units were also required to participate in the exercises. Many were not frontline troops. Men from the Air Forces and Navy took part.

The Naval Beach Battalions had the job of controlling movement to and from the beach. Pharmacists mate 3rd class, Vincent A. Kordcack, Platoon

B-6, Company B, 6th Naval Beach battalion, describes the experience from the perspective of one of these units during Exercise Fabius:

*April 24: After sleeping a few endless hours, we were awakened at 0405 to shoulder our gear and board the trucks. It was still dark when we arrived at Swansea, for it was only 0515 and dawn doesn't break till 0600. We were glad to get going for it was a misty morning and I started to get cold.*

*After sleeping for a few hours aboard train, we arrived at Dorchester. It was early afternoon, the time being 1410. We did not see anyone around the station even at this hour. But you could not expect to see many people in this part of England for everybody was north. From there, we went by truck convoy to our marshalling area. All the shelter we had here was a tent, cot and three blankets; this was what we were expected to keep warm with.*

*May 1: After we received a few points on the beach we were to hit, we studied maps of all types and they gave us the name of the town. It wasn't such a hot name, but everything over here is screwy. The name of the beach was Slapping (Slapton) Sands. The beach was composed of seashells and under this was sand, which was as tough as nails to work on. We left the marshalling area at 0500 by truck convoy. We had all of our gear with us, including one litter for each corpsman. We arrived at Weymouth at 0715 and found a beautiful sight in front of us. This place would be heaven for any liberty hound for there were plenty of service girls and civilians. We had a long walk along the beach before we boarded our ship. On the journey, we were given doughnuts and coffee for a pick up. When we arrived at the pier, they had an LCVP waiting to take us to our ship. When we arrived at the ship, they had nets for us to climb up on. It was an Army transport APA45. The name of the ship was the USS Henrico. We boarded ship at 1042 and lay below.*

*They did not have room for thirty of us so they put us in a hold below the water line. We had one advantage though and that was for chow for we were right below the chow hall. The chow was really delicious for it was the first Navy chow we had eaten for some time. They sold ice cream on board and that went like hot cakes since many had not tasted any for some time. It was the first time since my arrival in the United Kingdom. All that day we did nothing but stow our gear; we left port at 2000.*

*May 3:* *This was the big day of our problem; it was supposed to be the largest scale manoeuvre ever to have taken place. For us it is a good experience for it is the first time under actual fire. H-Hour was 0800 and I was topside early to see the beginning of the bombardment. They started to blast the beach at 0730 and it lasted for half an hour. It was really a sight to see, the guns working over that little piece of beach, especially the first time you see the real McCoy.*

*I had no worries for I did not have to go in till H+220 and by that time, most of the action would have cleared away from the beach. We finally lowered away in a Limey LCVP and started from our ship. But as we started towards shore, we had an accident. An LCT rammed us and the aft of our craft was destroyed. At first, we all thought we would have to go swimming but Turner told the coxswain to go back. Then we transferred to another Limey craft with very little difficulty. But that did not keep us from getting wet. We saw some other craft get hit as it was hard holding the landing formation since the water was rough. Our craft tossed around as though it was a piece of driftwood.*

*As we kept going in and arrived at the halfway mark, the darn thing went dead. If this had been the real thing with the Germans shelling us, I'm sure we would have not come back. But after all the misfortune that befell us, we finally hit the beach at H+4.*

*I threw my litter down and ducked for cover on the beach. After staying under cover for forty-five minutes, I started for the evacuation centre, which I found out was in an abandoned hotel. There I remained till I dried out. While there I saw a 'casualty' argue with an umpire about whether he was dead or not. If this had been the real thing, he would probably be arguing with St Peter not an Army captain.*

*Later I returned to the beach to pitch our pup tent. Jerry and I volunteered to take duty there. Our job was to watch the beach for anything that may turn up. This continued all day and part of the following day. The early part of May 4, we started bivouacking back in, over the hill. Here we stayed for the rest of the day and until 2200 of May 5. Then we took a truck convoy for Weymouth, which is only fifteen miles away. Then we took a train and started back for Dorchester. We arrived at 0700, after which, we took trucks to our marshalling area. This time we returned with our sea bags. Now we could go on liberty if we cared to do so.* [11]

The beaches at Slapton Sands were also used by some units to test new procedures. The firing of artillery from landing craft was part of the assault plan to maximise the bombardment of German positions during the run-in to the beaches. Land based artillery units do not normally practice this type of bombardment, so a new procedure had to be worked out. Lieutenant-Colonel Donald V. Bennett, 62nd Armored Artillery who were equipped with the M7 self-propelled 105mm howitzer, describes how they went about this:

*As we were going to be required to participate in the pre-H-Hour bombardment of the beach by firing our M7s from LCTs we asked if we could send A Battery down to Slapton Sands to try this out on an LCT borrowed from the British.*

*We mounted four M7s in the hull of the tank hold of the LCT, two up and two back. These LCTs were made in two halves and welded together. They had a centre line that went from the bow ramp all the way back through the bridge to the stern. We tied an aiming stake on the bow ramps, an extension of the centre line, then we laid all the pieces parallel to the centre line of the LCT, so we were able to fire the howitzers in the direction the LCT was pointing.*

*Now, we put the battery Exec up on the bridge, which is a narrow catwalk about six inches wide and he straddled the centre line. Previously we had picked aiming points on shore from aerial photos. Every time the aiming stake started coming across the aiming point, the battery Exec said 'Fire' and the gun with a round in the tube at that time fired. Then we had another man on each piece and all he did was keep the levelling bubble level. When the bow would go down he would crank the other way, just keeping the bubble level. We had another man on the range drum of each howitzer. We figured out that we were doing about five knots, which is 200 yards a minute. So we had a man on the bridge next to the battery Exec with one of these big dishpans that the army has in the kitchen kit and a wooden potato masher. Every thirty seconds another man with a stop watch would say 'Time' and then, wham the man would hit the dishpan and each piece decreased range by 100 yards.*

*Once in a while you could see where your shot was landing, since all we were doing was firing at the beach. If it 'walked' into the water, you would just add 200 yards to it; if it started 'walking' too far up the beach, you would drop 200. We did this, firing about 100 per piece on that exercise.*

*But the interesting part was that we didn't know what the LCT would stand. We started out with charge number one and it barely got over the bow. Finally, we settled on charge number five. We had seven charges on the 105mm howitzer at that time. When we fired all four pieces with charge five, that gave an awful jolt to the LCT. We could open up at about 9,500 yards offshore with charge five, thus we were going to be able to put an awful lot of fire on the beach.*

*I said, 'we're going to do it this way. Let's go in, we've done enough', and I went into the crew compartment of the LCT, which is just behind the tank hull compartment; just a steel plate separates it from where the M7s were. I was seated right up against the compartment at a table about fourteen inches wide, drinking a cup of coffee because I was frozen, it was so darn cold.*

*All of a sudden – Karoom! Everything came down on us and I went roaring out of there. It turned out that my battery commander couldn't stand that I hadn't tried out charge number seven and so after I had gone into the compartment, he loaded up those four pieces with charge seven and fired them. The LCT literally backed up in the water and we sprang about ten leaks. We started back towards the harbour since we were in the English Channel about 8,000 yards out at this time and we were sinking.*

*We had some of our gun crews manning the mechanical pumps, pumping as best we could. We went into Dartmouth River. We had gotten on the boat up near the Naval Academy but coming back we were about 400 yards from there and it was obvious we were going to sink before we got there, so we just put the boat into the shore.* [12]

Sergeant Roy Stevens, Company A, 1st Battalion, 116th Infantry Regiment, summed up his experience in a few words:

*Man Slapton Sands was tough. You realised very quick you had to stay down as low as you could to keep your head.* [13]

Some were more reflective. Pvt James 'Slim' James McCann, Company H, 2nd Battalion 506 PIR:

> *A few of us went off to Torquay and found a delightful hotel bar which had a curved window that gave a splendid view of the English Channel. We had the bar to ourselves as almost all the civilians had been cleared from the area. The usual boisterous drinking was absent. It was hard to believe, but we were in a contemplative mood and the conversation was subdued. Some of us talked about our upcoming journey across the Channel, while others just looked out lost in their own thoughts. Let's face it, we all knew that some of us were not going to return.[14]*

For some the training seemed endless and they just wanted it to end:

> *I'll be damned glad to get in there and get it over with, just to get a rest.[15]*

The end would soon come. The real Day of Days was beckoning.

## Chapter Twelve

# Exercise Tiger – Controversy and Conspiracy

Military Training is inherently dangerous. It involves not only the firing of weapons with live ammunition in as near as possible to combat conditions, but also involves training troops with equipment they may be unfamiliar with and in environments which may be unfamiliar. They will be working long hours under extreme pressure, often with little sleep. During wartime most soldiers will also be hostilities only, i.e. not regular professional soldiers and therefore not have benefited from a base level of experience gained from military service over a number of years. During wartime, whoever they are, they will all know that they will probably be doing it for real, in the near future. During training accidents are bound to happen, despite the toughest of safety procedures. This is particularly the case during wartime when safety has by necessity to be a lower priority in favour of added realism.

In my own experience, having been a historian specialising in the history of military training as well as a serviceman myself, I have tensional experience of such accidents. Whilst serving in Germany in 1979 a fellow soldier and friend was accidentally killed under tragic circumstances, as a result of being run over by a large military vehicle. Whilst working with the MOD in a historical capacity on military training areas, I have been present when fatalities and serious accidents have occurred. These can occur for a variety of reasons but many happen as a result of motoring accidents or from weapon training with live ammunition. I have been present during a live firing exercise when a soldier was accidentally shot on a field firing area nearby (luckily not fatal on this occasion). When training for actual war, the tempo of training is increased, along with the likelihood of accidents.

One of the key events associated with Slapton Sands was not a training accident, but took place as a result of enemy action.

During the night of 26–27 April 1944, during Exercise Tiger, a convoy of LSTs were en-route for Slapton sands to take part in Exercise Tiger. Convoy

T-4 consisted of LST-515, LST-496, LST-511, LST-531, LST-58 (which was towing two pontoon causeways), LST-499, LST-289, and LST-507, with the Flower-class corvette HMS *Azalea* providing escort. The convoy sailed from Plymouth at 9.45 am on 26 April and was proceeding in column with HMS *Azalea* in the lead. The convoy had already steamed past Slapton Sands, following a route that would take it north-eastwards along the coast. There it turned around off the coast of Dorset in Lyme Bay and looped back to Slapton Sands. The LSTs were carrying men of the US 1st Engineer Special Brigade who were planned to land their cargoes of men, vehicles and equipment on the beach as part of a follow-up wave. At 01.30 on 27 April the convoy was attacked by German fast motor torpedo S-boats. Sailing from Cherbourg the S-boats intercepted and attacked the convoy. As a result of the attack two of the LSTs (LST-507 and LST-531) were sunk and a third (LST-289) severely damaged. The official number of fatal casualties suffered as a result of this attack was 639 men. Many of those that survived were forced to endure a significant time in the freezing water before being eventually picked up. A number of bodies of those that had perished were also picked up. The survivors were sent to military hospitals. The bodies of the dead were temporarily interred at the Brookwood Military Cemetery in Surrey and later moved to the US Military cemetery at Cambridge (now known as the Cambridge American Cemetery and Memorial). In accordance with the policy of the United States the interment of the remains of war dead was carried out by the American Graves Registration Service. After the war the next of kin, were allowed to make the decision regarding interment. They could have chosen to have the remains returned to the United States for permanent interment at a national or private cemetery, or permanently interred at the overseas American military cemetery in the region where the death occurred. As a result, those that died in the Exercise Tiger attack are either buried at Cambridge or were later re-buried in the USA[1].

It is unfortunate but perhaps understandable that the story of the preparation for D-Day at Slapton Sands has often concentrated on the attack on convoy T-4 during the night of April 28 1944, at the expense of the real story of the Assault Training Area, which is its contribution to the success on 6 June 1944.

There are a number of misconceptions, conspiracy theories and much conjecture that relate to the events of that night. Some writers question the numbers of fatal casualties that occurred, and imply a cover-up by the US authorities.

The precise number of men that lost their lives as a result of the S-boat attack on convoy T-4 has been the subject of much conjecture over the years. Figures of between 639 and 749 are quoted[2]. One source claims that a significantly higher number than this is possible, but without any evidence. This source makes allusions to an official cover-up. Discrepancies are described in relation to the mismatching of certain dates and other information, and a small number of cases cited. The author quite rightly states that some may be due to inaccurate record keeping and misidentification, but a deliberate cause is concluded.

If you look hard enough for a conspiracy, then surely one will appear. This seems to be the case in relation to these theories. The cases cited lack sufficient detail or consistency to prove any deliberate cover-up.

There are also claims that hundreds of men were killed when fired on by their own side during practice landings.

Reference has been made to large numbers of men having been killed as a result of being shelled by warships firing as part of a naval bombardment during practice landings. Crew members of certain British ships claim that there were 'heavy casualties amongst the American lads who went ashore'.[3]

Despite no factual reference existing to prove this story from either ship or units ashore, this has not prevented major television channels promoting this story as fact. Two recent examples of this include the Channel 5 documentary, *The Secret D-Day Disaster: Revealed* and the Channel 4 progam, *D-Day as it Happens.*[4]

In relation to large-scale losses occurring as a result of other training activity, an unreferenced story is related by a sergeant of the 203rd Engineer Combat who whilst practicing lifting mines in an unnamed location 'saw bodies floating in on the tide'. The number of bodies is unknown and their identity unknown.

Another unreferenced story relates to 'local witnesses who had slipped through the perimeter security and entered the exercise area for unknown reasons' and had recalled 'seeing bodies on the shore at Blackpool Sands'. No number of casualties is revealed, and the dead are not identified.[5]

The English Channel during 1943 and 1944 was a war zone. Conflict was taking place both on the water as well as in the air. It was not unknown for bodies to be washed ashore from sunken ships of from crashed aircrew.

Coroner's records should record the finding of any such bodies, but unfortunately the records for South Devon prior to 1949 no longer exist.

No documentary or substantiated accounts exist to verify any of these types of event ever occurring[6]. It is certainly likely that some fatal casualties resulted from the training. This must be expected with the scale and type of training that took place. Author Alex Kershaw's excellent book, *The Bedford Boys,* describes the collective experience of the men of A Company 116th Infantry Regiment training at Slapton Sands and The Assault Training Center at Woolacombe and probably sums up the real situation that actually occurred. 'In Company A, there were minor injuries – sprained ankles, cuts, and bruised egos – but no serious casualty until one particularly cold day when Bedford Boy Andrew Coleman collapsed with pneumonia aggravated by the wet and cold conditions.'[7]

Also there are claims that large numbers of men killed were secretly buried on or near the Slapton Sands area as a result of being killed taking part in practice landings.

In 1984 a number of events swung the media spotlight of the events that took place on 26/27 April 1944. The local commercial television station TVS broadcast a documentary named *Sands of Silence* about the about the attack on the LSTs during Exercise Tiger. It was described as a 'sketchy account of the disaster' by Author Nigel Lewis in his book *Channel Firing,* but 'still the most comprehensive thus far'.

In May of 1984 another local resident, Ken Small, successfully concluded a long-running project to raise a Sherman DD amphibious tank that had been lost during practice landings.

In the same year a local resident, Dorothy Seekings, attracted considerable media attention claiming she had been given a lift by an American soldier in a lorry carrying 'stacks and stacks' of bodies that were buried locally in a field near the boundary of the training area. Needless to say, for the media this was a story too good to miss, regardless of any proven facts. This has led to a number of claims that the American soldiers killed as result of the Exercise Tiger incident were then secretly buried locally as part of a cover-up. These claims have been comprehensively disproved, as records exist to show that all the bodies recovered as a result of this incident were interred either at Brookwood or Cambridge[8].

The work of recording and managing battle casualties in the United States Army was the responsibility of Graves Registration Companies. An insight into the work of the 605th Graves Registration Company is given by topographic draughtsman Tech 5 Emmett Bailey jr, who took part in Exercise Tiger:

*While we were there, we were training to open graves and fill out forms necessary. This was done using some of our own personnel. We would open graves in a cow pasture or any assigned place, use our buddies as casualties, strip them of their ID such as dog tags and record all their details as if they were actual casualties. While we were in the process of doing this, the combat troops were holding exercises at Slapton Sands. One time we were opening some graves in the area of the 4th Infantry Division. Some of their units were walking by on a field march, and despite the fact that we had some tarpaulins to screen what we were doing, one of the men of the unit asked over the barrier what we were doing. Unfortunately, one of our personnel answered him that we were digging a grave for him – a most regrettable incident. He was reprimanded severely by all of us and our officer for having made this statement. Graves Registration had no special ID for our unit, other than the ones for the unit we were assigned to, like the 1st Infantry Division. We did not go around advertising what our mission was, particularly to combat troops, because it would have been injurious to their morale.*[9]

It was the 605th Graves Registration Company that took care of the bodies of the army men that were recovered from the sea as a result of the attack on the LSTs during Exercise Tiger. He further goes on to describe this:

*On April 28 1944, several German torpedo boats came out of Cherbourg and attacked a troop convoy. We collected the casualties – several hundred of them – and transported them to the old World War One cemetery that was at Brookwood, England, southwest of London. They were given full military honor burials. There were contracted morticians there. They placed the deceased on embalming tables and did what was necessary. We went through the ID process and put some new clothing on them. We took them out into a cemetery and they were interred.*[10]

Emmett Bailey also states, 'To my best memory, we did not participate in any burial of bodies other than from Exercise Tiger while we were in England.'[11] He also testifies that no mass burials took place for the men who died during Exercise Tiger and states: 'The claim that these casualties were buried in a mass grave was an insult to the integrity of our Graves Registration unit, because there was no mass burial in England'.[12]

Emmett Bailey's first-hand account gives an indication of how soldiers on exercise may have misinterpreted what they saw, confusing practice training with real burials. His testimony pertains to the 605th Graves Registration Company, the very unit that was responsible for the managing the army casualties from Exercise Tiger. Their job was to look after the remains of their dead comrades, a duty the Graves Registration units clearly took extremely seriously.

There is an oblique reference in the US Military history relating to Operation Neptune to 'unfortunate accidents'[13] relating to the forced use of additional fire support provided by artillery firing from landing craft due to a lack of naval gunfire support available during the assault phase of the landing. But the history does not expand on the meaning of this.

Whilst no formal documentary evidence exists to prove any large-scale loss of life occurred due to training accidents, there are some contemporary media references from late 1943.

*The Western Morning News* of 20 December 1943 features a short article titled 'US Army Exercise Some Soldiers Drowned in Craft Mishap':

American Army Exercises in England on Saturday (18th Dec) involved a number of casualties through mishaps to craft being used in amphibious practice. Along a stretch of Sands extending several miles, and where in peacetime surf-bathing is a popular pastime with holidaymakers, the United States Army has for some time been carrying out assault training.

On the occasion of a press visit to the centre recently, the Commanding officer, an American colonel spoke of the realistic nature of the training, and said casualties were inevitable. The mishap occurred within sight of persons on the shore and it is understood to have been caused by the condition of the sea at the time. Many soldiers were thrown into the water and some drowned.

*The Western Morning News* on the 29 December 1943 also reported:

US INVASION REHEARSAL
Biggest Manoeuvres
CASUALTIES IN LANDINGS
by Franklin Banker Associated Press War Correspondent
with US TROOPS IN ENGLAND Tuesday

In one of the biggest war manoeuvres ever held, battle-eager young American soldiers are getting practical training day and night for the forthcoming invasion of Western Europe under Gen. Eisenhower.

Naval forces and all kinds of army units, amphibious infantry, artillery, armoured units, and air forces, engineers and supply units are participating in the gigantic dress rehearsal.

**COAST AND INLAND**
The vast operations extend over a desolate stretch of coast and for miles inland. As in the real thing, troops and tanks stream ashore with naval and air support and seek to establish bridgeheads under gunfire.

Casualties naturally result and the troops are hardened to take these as part of war.

Members of an amphibious outfit for example reported that they suffered casualties from landing operation. A number of men were drowned when a flat-bottomed tank landing craft was upset by 20ft waves. Waves were so high that the drivers of 'ducks' were unable to see where they were going except when on the crest of a wave. Many men were drenched.

Despite their setback they worked next day in pouring rain to regrease the 'ducks'.

## 'ITS TOUGH'

'Yeah, it's tough, but that's the price of war,' said a 'duck' driver from North Carolina. 'What we want to do is to hustle over to the continent and get this invasion over with. Just show me the coast – that's all I ask.'

There is no direct reference to Slapton Sands in either news piece and the dates in respect of major assault training commencing are too early. The first major amphibious exercise, Duck I, did not commence until 4 January 1944. The likelihood is that the incident or incidents referred to happened not at Slapton Sands but at the Assault Training Centre at Woolacombe in North Devon as training here commenced in 1943.

Whilst the US, British and Canadians had different procedures, the Operation Order issued by the 3rd Canadian Infantry Division which participated in Exercise Trousers at Slapton Sands in April 1944 clearly details the procedures should a fatality occur during the exercise:

*If a death occurs during the Exercise it will in all cases be the responsibility of the Unit of the individual concerned to make the necessary arrangements for Courts of Inquiry, to contact the local civil authorities for inquest, to report the casualty to Headquarters 3 Canadian Infantry Division, and to make the burial arrangements.*

*The removal of the body of the deceased to the nearest mortuary will also be a unit responsibility at all times except after the unit has been broken up into craft loads or parties until the unit is re-assembled after landing.*

*While afloat it will be the responsibility of the Officer Commanding craft loads or parties. He will also be responsible for advising the Unit of the individual concerned of the particulars.*

*If death occurs before embarkation, Officer Commanding craft party will make arrangements with the static organisations to remove the body.*

*If death occurs after embarkation but before sailing Officer Commanding craft party will make arrangements with the Senior naval representative to have the body transported ashore with an escort of two men and an officer or senior NCO instructed to remove the body to the nearest mortuary and have the unit advised.*

*If death occurs after sailing and before the Unit of the individual concerned has been reassembled Officer Commanding craft party will deliver the body to an officer of the Beach Group who will be responsible for removing the body to the nearest mortuary and advising the unit of the particulars[14].*

Whilst no documented instructions exist from an equivalent document for a US exercise, it can be assumed that similar procedures would have been in place. Clear and concise instructions would be difficult to cover up, as numbers of individuals would require 'silencing' as well as the local civil authorities (the coroner) – an unlikely event.

Having grown up in the area local to Slapton Sands and having researched the subject for in excess of thirty years I have found absolutely no evidence to back up any of the 'conspiracy' theories. One has to conclude that there is neither firm basis nor documentary evidence to prove any of them. First-hand evidence, where it does exist, is, in every case, uncorroborated.

Undoubtedly, there were fatal training accidents. Training on the scale that took place would surely have led to some fatalities, but there is no credible or substantiated proof, either that large-scale casualties occurred at Slapton Sands or Blackpool Sands, or that any burials ever occurred in the Slapton Sands area.

## Chapter Thirteen

# Handing Back

Now that the exercises had been completed, and the area was no longer required for training the question of de-requisitioning and handing the area back had to be addressed.

The local residents, whilst being keenly aware of what had been taking place in the area, had known little of the detail of what had happened. Some of those living in the district commented that they had witnessed a tank battle one day from a hilltop but that they had really seen and heard very little of what was going on in the prohibited area. One local resident Mrs I. Clements, whose home was at Stokenham and whose husband was a builder and had a business in Stokenham, described how they used to watch the red flag which was flown as a warning over the battle training area: 'When we did not see it for some weeks we began to hope … Then we saw coloured troops going in to the area and we knew that our return could not be yet and then we heard the official news.'[1]

As early as 30 April 1944, the Commander-in-Chief Plymouth, Admiral Leatham, had raised the question of considering what plans should be made for the time when the Slapton Assault Training Area would no longer be required by the American Forces.

It was on 8 July 1944 that the chief of Staff, SHAEF, Lt. Gen. Walter Bedell Smith had confirmed to Allied Naval Commander-in-Chief Expeditionary Force (ANXCF) Admiral Sir Bertram H. Ramsay that, 'provided the Studland Assault Training Area is kept available for the use of either US or British units/formations and the Woolacombe area is retained for the use of US forces. There is no objection to the release of all other assault training areas. ANXCF would not require the Slapton Sands area for any purpose… therefore the area could be returned to the civilians as soon as it could be made fit for occupation.'[2]

Within the British Government, the usual arguments started in relation to whose responsibility it was to reinstate the area and who was going to pay for it. Different responsibilities potentially lay with different agencies, with the Treasury ultimately holding the purse strings.

Amongst the Government departments that could be responsible were the Ministry of Works, the War Office, the Admiralty and the Ministry of Agriculture. It was decided however that the Admiralty was to be responsible: 'Since the Admiralty insisted on doing the requisitioning they must deal with the reinstatement.'[3]

The Treasury had formally recognised that the reinstatement of the area was to be treated as a special case. The government would be required to enable the evicted communities to move back and resume their occupations. Additionally it was recognised that the US Army had benefited so much from the training carried out in the Slapton area that it should do all it could to help.

The process of reinstatement was to be broken down into three categories: land, public utilities and buildings.

In the case of the land where military use had not been prolonged or severe, farmers themselves were expected to deal with restoration of their land and claim compensation for doing it. Arrangements would be made to help and to find material – i.e. fences, etc. Where the productiveness of land had been temporarily destroyed and the farmer could not deal with himself, then the Ministry of Agriculture would be responsible for reinstating the fertility of the soil.

Restoration of public utilities would be the responsibility of the Ministry of War Transport and the Ministry of Health. It was agreed that due to the exceptional nature of the evacuation, it would be unreasonable to simply derequisition the area, pay compensation and leave people to their own devices.

In relation to buildings, where these had been totally destroyed the Government would not rebuild, but would pay monetary compensation. For buildings that were repairable but uninhabitable, they too would be repaired by owners themselves, who could then claim compensation. The Treasury however would only pay to make properties 'reasonably habitable' and not to reinstate them to their exact condition prior to requisition. It was explained that this would be wasteful of labour and possibly 'involve the Government in greater expense than the proper monetary compensation which was to be defined as appropriate'.[4]

A shortage of labour was identified as a major problem. Labour was anyway in short supply, but this was exacerbated at the time due to Flying Bomb attacks which had caused a great demand for building materials and labour.

A meeting held with local farmers in July 1944 provided some welcome news for the authorities. The farmers indicated that they considered that not as much reconditioning as had previously been thought was required and that they were, generally speaking, anxious to do their own restoration.

A formal meeting to discuss the de-requisition and handing back was held on 4 July 1944 at the SHAEF Headquarters at Norfolk House in St James Square, London.[5] It was chaired by Sir Findlater Stewart, with General Sir Hugh Elles the Regional Commissioner present and representatives from various agencies that would be involved. At the meeting it was agreed that many facilities including post, foodstuffs, coal and petrol stocks, stocks of civilian consumption goods, electricity, transport services, and sewage repairs would also need to be considered. These would be managed by the various departments concerned. Road repair would in the first place be the responsibility of the local authority (Devonshire County Council), assisted by the Ministry of Transport. As the requisitioning authority, the Admiralty was responsible for the reinstatement. It would ultimately be responsible for ensuring that damage to farmland, buildings and hedges, etc would be made good, but that other departments would assist, acting as their agents in the provision of materials and labour. The resources of the regional and local authorities would also be made available to help.

It was in the national interest to secure the speediest return of farmers to this valuable agricultural area. The Admiralty would be responsible for informing farmers that they would be allowed to return at an early date and that the remainder of the population would return as soon as their houses could be made reasonably habitable. A local timetable for reoccupation was to be drawn up and the date for handing over to the civil police was agreed with the Chief Constable of Devon.

The area was to be certified clear of unexploded shells and other dangers to life as soon as possible, but this could not be done before a thorough search had been made and might take until 1 August 1944.

The Americans would do all they could to rehabilitate the area.

The restoration carried out by government action was to extend only so far as ensuring that houses were reasonably habitable and that land was reasonably restored. The balance of other minor repairs was to be met by compensation claims.

It was formally agreed that Slapton Sands Assault Training Area was no longer required for military or naval assault training.

As with the evacuation, information centres were once more set up in the area to provide advice to residents. One of the key elements was the arrangement of transport for people, possessions, livestock and equipment back to the area. The local transport industry had played a big part in the evacuation when time, weather and the hours of daylight were all against them. Now they would play an equally important part in helping people return. To ensure that transport could be arranged with as little delay as possible, an advisory committee was set up and an office opened at 11 Mill Street in Kingsbridge.[6]

Amongst the first to enter the area officially were representatives of the Kingsbridge Rural District Council and the press. A tour of the area was organised and on 29 July 1944 a reporter from the *Western Morning News* described the scene:

*No smoke curls from the chimneys. No cat washes itself on the cottage doorstep. No hen clucks in the backyard and no sleek cattle graze the overgrown fields.*

*Not a sound disturbs the unnatural silence of the south Devon evacuation area which a couple of months ago was the scene of fierce mock battles by means of which our American allies prepared themselves for the invasion of Normandy.*

*Roses cascade over walls of the deserted homes and fruit ripens unpicked and drops to the ground from bushes in gardens where nature has been allowed to run riot.*

*Badly scarred but still lovely is the rural area to which the inhabitants, who were bundled out bag and baggage last Christmas, have been told they may soon return.*

*Miles of glass will be required to replace the shattered windows, few of which remain intact, and much clearing up and repair work will have to be done before the people who are looking forward to it with joyous anticipation will be able to return.*

*It is obvious that the Americans have taken such care as was possible. The damage is extensive, although in some of the village it is mainly superficial.*

*This cannot be said of all the area. For example the hills overlooking the east end of Slapton Sands look as if a hurricane has swept over them. Apparently having come under heavy shellfire from the sea the trees have been blasted and stripped of their foliage and the wall edging the roadway no longer exists in many places, while below, the seaside houses have been destroyed.*

*Ferocious battles have raged along the coast where road and sand have been churned up by the passage of heavy vehicles and concrete roadblocks, and strong-points have been thrown down by the weight of the shells directed at them and here and there on the edge lie broken and useless landing craft.*

*Although all the churches and chapels are marked 'out of bounds' and have been marked in an attempt to safeguard them from bomb and shell, at least one of them at Slapton has suffered considerable damage.*[7]

The area nearest the beaches where the assault training had taken place had sustained significant damage. The Royal Sands Hotel on the beach opposite the road to the village of Slapton had been virtually destroyed along with Strete Gate Manor, another large building near the beach but at the western end of the beach. The road leading from Strete to the beach area featured a stone wall. This had large sections that had been damaged by shellfire. A mile inland, Stokenham had also sustained some damage, but it had been on a lesser scale. The Church had escaped with some damage to the slate roof, but the nearby public house, the Church House Inn, had been badly damaged inside and out. At Torcross and Chillington there was less damage and those villages furthest away from the beach had sustained the least damage.

Mr G.C.N. Mackarness, regional information officer representing the Regional Commissioner Sir Hugh Elles, commented: 'Some houses in some cases were not what they once were but the smallness of damage was remarkable considering the nature of the exercises carried out.' The actual number of buildings totally destroyed or severely damaged in the Slapton and Strete area was few. Elsewhere throughout the area the damage was mainly superficial and limited to broken windows and door hinges. Mr Mackarness stated that 'by and large, I think everyone who has been through the area has been surprised by the lightness of the damage.'[8]

It is a remarkable testament to those controlling the bombardments during the assault exercises that so little damage was done to the villages in the area, areas that had been clearly designated as valid for live fire activity, both on the beaches and in the hinterland. But on the beach itself it was clearly not possible to avoid structures within areas under preparatory bombardment. The nature of naval bombardment from sea to shore includes a certain level of probable error. It was these occasional 'overs' that most likely caused the damage.[9]

The impact of the land through lack of maintenance had led to grass being knee high on lawns and in the fields. Vegetation throughout the area was generally overgrown. Some unused roads had become overgrown with lack of use. Damage had occurred to roads, with some hedges having been knocked down. People arriving back in the villages found that some places were overrun by rats. When windows were eventually replaced, the putty, which included fish oil as a constituent, had been eaten by the rats.[10] Special mobile squads of rat catchers were employed.[11]

Around 1,000 American troops were engaged in making the area safe. They had begun with the clearance of explosives, miles of barbed wire, and shells had that been dumped in and around the Slapton area. The troops performing the clearance were reported as having been very careful and had gone over the same land twice, but it was recognised that it was going to be a long job before a certificate of safety could be issued.

Whilst many were looking forward to returning to the area, some would choose not to. They had experienced for the first time the amenities of electric light and water and did not wish to return to oil lamps and pump water, which were the amenities that would await them on their return to the evacuated area. However everything possible was done to restore services. Amongst the first to return were GPO workers, to repair damaged telephone lines.

*Chapter Fourteen*

# Slapton Sands Today

For a visitor to the evacuated area of the South Hams today, the impact of the practice assault exercises is largely unnoticeable. The beach area at Slapton Sands has remained very much the same as it did in 1944. But a major area of change is the beach foreshore. Here, erosion has pushed back the edge of the beach right back towards the main A379 road between Strete and Torcross.

Two main features in the Slapton Sands beach area that commemorate the practice landings today are the Sherman DD tank recovered from the sea, and the memorial to those who left their homes so that the area could be used for battle practice.

## The Sherman DD Tank

Displayed in the main visitor car park at Torcross is a Sherman M4 DD tank that was lost during assault practice training in 1944. Although the tank itself had been lost, no crewmembers lost their lives and the tank lay at the bottom of the sea off the beach at Torcross, forgotten by all but a few, for many years. The tank belonged to Company A of the 70th Tank Battalion and had sunk during a training exercise along with another tank. The other tank was recovered at the time, but one remained where it sank, on the seabed[1].

Captain Harry C. Butcher USNR, a naval aide to the supreme commander General Dwight Eisenhower recalls the sinking of a DD Tank during Exercise Tiger:

*Ike and his party boarded LCI(L) 495 at 6 in the morning... I had gone aboard LCI(L) 487 with Scarman and Reid, as well as other members of an official party from SHAEF, including Major Generals Harold R. Bull and Robert W. Crawford. We reached our observing position as the naval bombardment of strong points on the shore was begun. H-Hour was to have been at 7:30 a.m. unless the weather was so bad the aircraft could not participate, in which event it was to have been at 7 o'clock. As the naval bombardment started on schedule and the weather seemed perfect, with a smooth sea, we assumed H-Hour was 7:30 as advertised. The LCTs bearing waterproofed tanks called DDs were in position to be launched at 7:15. These are the tanks which, with canvas waterproofing, proceed to shore under their own propulsion. They have propellers.*

*Then there was a delay in the landing; why, we did not know, although later we heard that H-Hour had been postponed even after the naval bombardment had begun for one hour. This left LCTs and their cargoes of DDs (tanks that float) milling around, waiting. In due time, the DDs were successfully launched and slowly made their way toward the beach at three or four knots an hour. One, I noticed, was smoking. It had proceeded about a mile somewhat parallel to the beach when I saw a yellow object pushed from the tank. I first thought this was a marker buoy, but soon realized it was a dinghy and that the tank was in trouble. Soon an LCVP sped toward it. In a few moments, the tank crew was in the yellow dinghy and the tank had sunk. This was the only tank casualty and, fortunately, no one was lost.*

It is not known if the tank that Captain Butcher witnessed sinking is the tank recovered, but the likelihood would seem high that it might well have been.[2]

Tank units equipped with DD tanks were based and trained at Torcross. This training was carried out under the direction of Colonel Severne S. McLaughlin, the US Third Armored Group Commander. To keep secret the nature of this training, the area selected was sufficiently far removed from Slapton Sands to avoid observation by the remainder of the troops. The DD tank training consisted of teaching the tank crews to launch their tanks and using the duplex drive to drive them ashore under their own power on the surface of the water. Once ashore, they abandoned their buoyancy equipment and proceeded as normal tanks.[3]

Staff Sergeant E. Gibson of Company A, 70th Tank Battalion, to whom the lost tanks belonged, explains the concept of how the tanks were used:

*The DD tank was a regular M-4, except it had a canvas screen that was raised by pneumatic pillars located around a false deck, which had been welded around the tank. These pillars were raised by two compressed air cylinders, which the driver controlled in his compartment. To raise the screen, the command was 'Driver inflate'. The screen was then inflated by pillars located around the tank. After the screen was inflated, there were 'struts' located fore and aft around the sides that had to be locked in place to keep the canvas screen from collapsing when the tank was launched.*

*The tank was self-propelled by two three-bladed propellers that were geared to rear idlers attached to the tracks in the rear. Commands to move the tank forward in the water were 'Driver lower propellers and advance in third gear'. This turned the tracks, which in turn rotated the propellers, moving the tank forward. After arrival on the beach, the commands were 'Driver raise propellers' which was done hydraulically, then 'Driver break struts', which was also done hydraulically. Then the driver deflated the screen by a mushroom valve located at the bottom of the pillars. At this time the screen had fallen and we had an M-4 medium tank on the beach ready to fight.*

He continues by describing what happened to the battalion in England after its arrival in Swindon:

*There we were issued medium M-4 tanks. We trained on them for several months. We trained at Swindon and Castle Martin Range in Wales. Then we moved to Portsmouth, where we trained on the British Valentine DD (duplex drive) tank. This training was on a completely camouflaged freshwater lake. After this we moved to Torcross, England on the channel shore and were issued M-4 DD tanks. These had to be completely waterproofed. All tanks had to be camouflaged with shrimp nets during the day. Torcross was completely off limits to anyone except Companies A and B of the 70th Tank Battalion. Our mess supplies were brought to a designated point, where they were picked up by our mess sergeants. No one could leave the Torcross beach area while training here, but we had excellent food. We had many night training missions, where we were loaded on LCTs at night and taken five to ten miles out in the channel and given a compass bearing (we had a compass on the tank) from the LCT skipper so as to head back to the beach at Torcross.*[4]

Corporal Wardell Hopper of Company B, 741st Tank Battalion also recalls this training:

*We went to Torcross, England; it was beautiful. It was just about like the beaches of Omaha. We trained there and took the M-4s out into the water. Our equipment and training were supposed to be top secret. The training was totally on the coast. We had some classroom instruction, but not much. They took us out in an LCT and then we went back in. We trained in the water in the swimming pool in case something happened to the tank. We trained in the pools on what to do if our tanks went down. They threw us into the water and we inflated our Mae Wests with capsules.*

*We put the skirt up a couple of times to test it, but not many times. You had it up before you launched it from the LCTs. All four tanks had the skirts up and motors on before launching. We didn't make many practices using the skirts up.*[5]

In 1984 the tank was recovered from the sea to act as a memorial to those men who lost their lives in Lyme Bay whilst on their way to participate in Exercise Tiger. A remarkable local resident, Ken Small, drove the recovery. Mr Small had fought British bureaucracy and, after being helped to purchase the tank for a token $50 by the owners of the tank, the American Government, he set about organising the recovery. This required a diving ship, recovery divers, bomb disposal, and a heavy recovery capability, not to mention arranging matters with the local authority, and taking measures to preserve the tank, which had spent decades under water. On Friday 18 May, thanks to Ken Small and his recovery team, the tank at last reached the beach, something that it had failed to do forty years earlier.

Since then the tank has formed a focal point for a number of memorials and provides an important reminder to visitors to the area today of the practice assaults that took place in the area during 1944. It remains a fitting testament not only to those who lost their lives during the D-Day practice landings, but to Ken Small himself, who passed away in March 2004.

## The Memorial

In recognition of the contribution of those who gave up their homes and lands to allow the assault training to take place, the US Army Authorities erected a twenty foot high monument at Slapton Sands. The obelisk, made of Devon granite, is located on the beach at the centre of Slapton Sands. The inscription on the memorial reads:

> THIS MEMORIAL WAS PRESENTED BY THE UNITED STATES ARMY AUTHORITIES TO THE PEOPLE OF THE SOUTH HAMS WHO GENEROUSLY LEFT THEIR HOMES AND THEIR LANDS TO PROVIDE A BATTLE PRACTICE AREA FOR THE SUCCESSFUL ASSAULT IN NORMANDY IN JULY 1944.
>
> THEIR ACTION RESULTED IN THE SAVING OF MANY HUNDREDS OF LIVES AND CONTRIBUTED IN NO SMALL MEASURE TO THE SUCCESS OF THE OPERATION.
>
> THE AREA INCLUDED THE VILLAGES OF BLACKAWTON CHILLINGTON EAST ALLINGTON SHERFORD SLAPTON STOKENHAM STRETE AND TORCROSS TOGETHER WITH MANY OUTLYING FARMS AND HOUSES.

The idea for a memorial was actually formed before the war had ended, with discussions being held in early 1945. The memorial was officially dedicated on Sunday 8 July 1945 in the presence of more than 500 people. The commanding general of the US communications zone (Lieutenant-General John C. Lee) presented the monument to the chairman of the Devon County Council (Sir John Daw).

'Our soldiers, sailors and airmen came here to train for the fight of their lives,' said General Lee in his speech at the ceremony. 'Many gave their lives and far more would have fallen never to rise again, but for the sacrifice which was made by you people. As an American soldier, I salute you, the unseen army, the army who made this great sacrifice without ribbons, without service stripes and without hope of reward.' General Lee added that between December 1943 and June 1944 thousands of American troops were trained in the Slapton Sands area where they found the 10-mile stretch of Devon coastline to be almost an exact replica of the Normandy beaches. 'By learning the characteristics of this terrain and determining in advance the weapons and tactics which would be required to wrest loose a strongly entrenched enemy, we saved thousands of lives and, to a very real degree, ensured that D-Day would be the end of the long battle against Hitler. In the years to come many Americans will visit this historic area and I hope they will appreciate as keenly as we appreciate now the vital part you played in the preparation for the Battle of Europe.'

The US Navy's thanks were expressed by the officer commanding amphibious bases in the United Kingdom (Captain R.B. Hunt) who said: 'This monument is our token for what you inspiringly did for us. This stone will be a reminder to future generations of your unselfish generosity. It is our appreciation for what all England and you did for us.'[5] Also in attendance were Mr R.W. Prowse, Chairman of Kingsbridge Rural District Council and Earl Fortescue, Lord Lieutenant of Devon. The ceremony concluded with the American and British national anthems played by the 71st United States Navy Band and with cheers for General Lee and for British and American cooperation.

On the night of 11/12 January 2001, a combination of high tides and easterly gales caused severe erosion to the shingle ridge at Slapton Sands where the monument stood. The monument was seriously undermined by the storm and required repair. During these repairs the opportunity was also taken to add the village of Sherford to the inscription which had inadvertently been omitted from the original. This necessitated the removal of every one of the lead letters and carving back of the face of the granite monument to erase all trace of them. Each letter was then recast and refixed to seamlessly include the additional wording. The rededication ceremony took place on 13 November 2002, this being the 59th anniversary of the day in 1943 when the villagers of Slapton and the surrounding areas were first evacuated.

To the casual eye, the area shows few traces of the activities that took place in 1944.

As has been previously mentioned, some of the original beach defences had been used as targets during the assault practices. Amongst them were traditional concrete or concrete/brick pillboxes. These were located around the beach area and many were extant until certainly the 1990s and possibly the early years of the 21st Century. Behind the beach on the far shore of the Higher Ley opposite Hartshorn plantation, the damaged remains of a pillbox stood for many years. During the 1970s I remember digging out the steel core of a .50 machine gun bullet, which had embedded itself in the concrete of the structure. At the Strete Gate end of the beach on the high ground in front of Coleridge Place there were two more pillboxes. The highest was of mixed brick and concrete construction and had been badly damaged. Another concrete structure was located further down from the higher pillbox. This had also suffered from a direct hit. The front had been blown in causing the roof to collapse and slope downwards. It was still however possible to enter the bunker via some steps. Sadly, little or none of these structures now remain. A larger bunker was believed to have been located just off Sands Road in the fields near the bridge over Slapton Ley. This is thought to have been demolished shortly after the war and a hut used for bird watching is located on or near the site.

Careful inspection of some of the fields in the area that have never been ploughed can reveal the remains of two man foxholes dug by the troops during the exercises.

Another tangible reminder is a large concrete block located in a field beside the rough track between Strete Gate and Homelands at the eastern end of the beach. Its original use is unknown. Strike marks from small arms ammunition can be seen on it.

Areas that were used as training areas for temporary periods only, often feature only ephemeral structures. Traces of these often disappear completely, become invisible to the eye, and can often only be rediscovered using archaeological techniques. Archaeological projects focusing particularly on conflict are now being widely carried out on First World War and Second World War sites. These projects often uncover information and previously unknown facts.

In 2005, an area of First World War training trenches dug by Australian troops was excavated on Salisbury Plain. Little was known about how training trenches had been constructed. Here it was discovered that the trenches dug by the Australians in hard chalk were only representative and not completely authentic as had been previously thought, as it was discovered that they were far too shallow to represent actual trenches as constructed on a real battlefield. (*Before the Storm: The Australian 3rd Division on Salisbury Plain in the First World War*, Richard Osgood, Martin Brown and Lucie Hawkins, Defence Estates).

Part of the original early war defence features included two scaffolding beach booms, officially known as Admiralty scaffolding or Obstacle Z1. One section was located at the centre of the beach opposite the road bridge to Slapton village, the other at the end of the road covering the beach exit to Strete. They were used during the assault training as obstacles. The rusting tubular framework was finally removed in November 1950 by contractors. During periods of dry weather when the water levels in Slapton Ley drop, some of the remains of this beach scaffolding can be seen on the near shore side, evidently dumped there after it was taken down.

Prior to the assault exercises, few buildings were located on the beach foreshore itself. The Royal Sands Hotel located at the centre of the beach near the road to Slapton village was built 1831 and used to be a favourite with sporting and hunting enthusiasts who enjoyed its proximity to the Ley. This was completely destroyed during the period of the exercises and is now the site of a car park. At the Strete Gate end of the beach a manor house had existed. This too was also damaged beyond repair during the exercises. For many years the site remained overgrown. Close examination of existing structures still provided evidence of the exercises in the form of shell fragment damage and bullet strike marks. Buildings on the opposite side of the road related to the larger house still exist and have now been turned into a luxury dwelling with a walled garden behind.

Examination of walls in the beach area, particularly those bordering the A379 on the high ground approaching the beach, show signs of damage and subsequent repairs.

The beach foreshore has been steadily eroding since the war. This erosion occasionally turns up reminders of the exercises in the form of spent cartridge cases and rusting shell fragments.

Two causeway bridges were built over the Higher Ley as part of the assault training. Whilst no obvious tangible evidence remains of these, examination of film footage taken during the exercises clearly shows the location of these bridges. Additionally, aerial photos clearly show the two spurs of land where the most westerly causeway bridge was built.

One of the lasting legacies of the assault raining is the presence of unexploded ordnance. Large amounts of live ammunition were fired during the practice assaults. This included naval bombardment, the firing of tanks and artillery from landing craft during the run in to the beach, and troops firing their personal and support weapons. Accounts from those that returned to the area soon after it had been handed back often tell of the amount of live ammunition still lying around the area despite the clearance work that had already been carried out. The nature of the countryside must have made recovery of unexploded items during the clearance particularly difficult. The area includes woodland, gorse and an abundance of natural cover, exacerbated at the time by lack of maintenance.

The shifting levels of the beach shingle by tidal or storm activity, often uncover unexploded ordnance. Problems began to come to light not long after the war. In May 1950 it was feared that part of Slapton Beach may have to be closed because live mines had been coming to the surface. The mines were un-fused, i.e. did not have the detonating mechanism fitted and could not have functioned if disturbed, but they still contained explosive. It was stated at the time that War Office representatives had examined the mines and closure was under consideration, but there was no need to alarm the public unduly.[7]

Later in November 1950, 127 objects were removed from the Slapton Sands foreshore. The Kingsbridge Rural District Council Chairman Mr R.W. Prowse stated that, 'it was a mercy no one had been killed at this stretch of sands. Thousands of people had walked over that part of the coast during the summer holidays in the past five years'.[8]

A letter to the editor of *The Western Morning News* at the time described how the beach had been cleared of British defensive mines before battle training took place, but 'was then resown for purposes of battle-training with American mines, live, but most of them un-fused. Thereafter over a period of months, the beach and the whole area behind it was liberally sprayed with explosive missiles of all descriptions, which inevitably included the usual proportion of 'blinds'. Lastly United States troops passing through the country dropped or otherwise left behind them a quantity of explosive items ranging from SA ammunition to large packages of TNT.

'After D-Day clearance parties of United States sappers worked for months on the beaches and over 30 square miles of farmlands. The area to be covered, the presence on the beach of much miscellaneous metal (each piece being picked up by the earphones), and the waist-high growth of weed inland were only some of the factors which made the task one of great difficulty and complexity'. The writer then comments that 'I do not think the authorities will ever be able to give an "all-clear" certificate in the sense of a guarantee that no explosive matter lies hidden in the area.'[9]

Whilst many types of unexploded ordnance have been and continue to be found today, one of the common types uncovered are British 5-inch High Explosive Rockets. The 'Gunfire Support Group 11th Amphibious Force' were amongst those that manned the specially converted landing craft who fired these rockets. Designated LCT(R) – Landing Craft Tank (Rocket) – these converted LCTs were designed to lay down an intensive barrage just prior to the landing of the initial assault waves.

Lieutenant (jg) L.W. Carr USN served with the Gunfire Support Group and describes how these rockets were used:

*The Gunfire Support Group was, effectively, an experiment in a new type of naval warfare. The need for close inshore fire support for landing operations had been identified in past amphibious invasions. Heavy naval gunfire from cruisers, destroyers etc., while effective at direct and indirect targets, had to be lifted from the beaches once the infantry had landed, whereas converted landing craft, aided by their shallow draught, could go close into beaches to fire on enemy positions. This close quarter support for landing troops was vitally important. The LCTRs were converted British Mk3 LCTs. An extra deck was constructed over the tank space and on it were mounted either 972 or 1044 5" rocket projectiles. The craft were equipped with 970 Radar, a British set which swept 360 degrees in azimuth once a second. The maximum range of the set was 25 miles. The primary use of the radar was ranging in the firing of the rockets but it proved to be a valuable navigation aid. The 5" rockets were fired electronically by a series of switches in the wheelhouse. Each switch would fire either 39 or 42 rockets per salvo, depending on the total number mounted. One group of 36 rockets was wired so that twelve salvos of three rockets could be fired for ranging. All projectors were mounted at a 45 degree angle to the waterline and all pointed forward. The target area was covered by pointing the craft's head at the target, determining the range by radar and/or ranging salvos. The firing of salvos with a pre-determined time interval between them gained the desired depth of pattern. The width of the pattern was 700 yards and could not be adjusted. The depth of a complete broadside of 24 salvos could be achieved within the range of 300 to 1,000 yards or even more if required. .... The proximity of our own troops approaching the beaches elevated the timing of a rocket barrage to the highest importance. Experience proved that rockets could be safely fired when the leading assault wave was some 700 yards from the beach or the point of impact of the rocket pattern. There were differences between the British and American use of the LCTRs off Normandy. The British fired at H–Hour minus 10 minutes while the American LCTRs fired at H–Hour minus 2 minutes at targets slightly inland.'[10]*

Two LCT(R)s had taken part in Exercise Duck II and created a good impression, even though one had released its rockets far too early. Nonetheless, they proved to American observers that the rocket was a weapon which could pulverise a sector of beach in the final few seconds before troops went ashore. During April 1944 LCT(R)s also took part in 'Exercise Tiger'. They were however not allowed to fire on the beaches because isolated units of the first wave had landed an hour before H–Hour due to a communications failure. LCT(R)s also took part in exercise Fabius 1. The original plan was that the LCTRs were to open fire when 300 yards from the shore, but this was later deemed to be too close for safety. Some difficulty was experienced by some of the craft taking part causing them to not be able to engage targets. Three craft successfully fired off their volleys and demonstrated once again the effectiveness of the rocket fire, which completely obliterated their theoretical targets.

The Gunfire Support Group continued to practice at Slapton Sands to bring new crews that had recently arrived with new craft up to operational standard with a series of firing exercises. Emphasis was placed on timing and accurate ranging using test salvos and radar.

Lieutenant Carr summarises the pros and cons of the LCT(R)s:

*The craft had several deficiencies. Extreme accuracy in navigation and a very steady course was essential during a firing run. Rudders were very small and the rocket racks increased the free board and made the craft more subject to the wind. 'Aiming the ship' was the only way to aim the rockets and more manoeuvrability would have been desirable. The LCTRs nevertheless, proved to be an effective and efficient weapon.*[11]

Captain Edward F. Wozenski, E Company, 16th Infantry, 1st Division remembers the LCT(R)s firing during exercises at Slapton Sands:

*I can recall back to the days at Slapton Sounds [sic] in England when we were rehearsing. We had nine Landing Ship Rockets. They would trigger off a rocket at a time until [one] walked on the water and hit the beach. Then somebody would pull the master switch and a thousand rockets would take off per ship. In a fantastic display, they just churn up the beach.*[12]

An early report of one of these projectiles coming to light was reported in *The Western Morning News* on 24 March 1950:

*While walking on Slapton Sands, Mr Maurice Lawson, postmaster of Torcross, noticed a thin piece of iron projecting from the beach. He walked over and gave it a tap. Failing to dislodge it, he cleared away the shingle. He then uncovered a 3ft long rocket, which may have been fired by American troops during their invasion training. With the assistance of an RAC scout, who was passing along the nearby main road, he carried the missile to the roadside and informed the police. They in turn called a bomb disposal squad from Devonport, which found it fully charged and with the fuse in perfect order. 'I never gave a thought to the risk of it being charged,' said Mr Lawson, 'but I felt differently when I heard that it was. After all,' he added with a smile, 'these things go off only once.'*[13]

These types of projectiles continue to be uncovered, which is perhaps not surprising. The three craft taking part in Exercise Fabius alone could in theory have fired up to 3,132 rockets.

So in truth, the Sherman DD tank and the memorial to the evacuated are not quite the only reminders of the assault exercises carried out at Slapton Sands. It seems likely that the discovery of unexploded ordnance may also continue to be a reminder of those dangerous and hectic days in 1944 for some years to come.

# Letters Sent to Those Evacuated with Regard to Claiming Compensation

## CIVIL DEFENCE
## OFFICE OF THE REGIONAL COMMISSIONER

Phone. No: Bristol 23346                   South Western Regional Office,
Telegrams: EMREGCOM, BRISTOL              19, Woodland Road,
                                                      BRISTOL, 8.
                                                 22nd April, 1944

Dear

Slapton Area Evacuation

Since the evacuation I have anxiously considered the subject of the effect on those who came within the scope of the order.

As you have been already advised, the scale of compensation for land and houses requisitioned in the evacuation area is limited by the Compensation Defence Act 1939, and it is legally impossible to award compensation at higher rates or on other grounds than those permitted by the Act.

An amendment of the law has been considered. But it has not been found practical politics to give the inhabitants of this area more favourable conditions than have been applied to the many thousands of persons elsewhere whose property has been requisitioned for purposes connected with the war.

Few of us have come unscathed through this war – for many the price has been their lives, for some the loss of everything they possessed. It has befallen the people in this area to be evacuated under conditions, which in many cases have involved them in financial loss. I have failed to find any source from which the loss can be made good. This must be accepted. On the other hand it is fully appreciated by all of us who have had any hand in dealing with the matter that the clearance of the area for military purposes has meant for numbers of the inhabitants not alone financial loss, but actual hardship and distress. When the United States Army authorities were approached, they indicated a desire to do everything possible to alleviate the hardship, which resulted from the evacuation of this area. An investigation disclosed that their laws, like ours would not permit the recognition of any legal claim for compensation. But the theatre Commander of the United States Army has generously made available to me a substantial sum of money to deal with special hardship cases. The fund is limited and is intended for those whose need is greatest. It is not meant to be distributed as an addition to the compensation, which has been awarded, and pecuniary loss cannot in itself justify a claim on the fund. It will be necessary to show distress and a serious lowering of the standard of living. It is also a condition that the fund should not be applied to cases where help is forthcoming from other sources such as supplementary pensions or grants from the Assistance board, which is the recognised authority for making payments in the nature of compensation to those who find themselves in need as a result of war.

I have appointed a special committee to decide on the allocation of the fund, to whom you may with every confidence submit any claim you may think you have to participate and who, I am sure, will give every consideration to those intimate details affecting your claim, which need to be dealt with confidentially.

The committee will consist of Sir John Daw. Major E.E Rives of the United States Army. Mr. K.G.Harper of the Regional Commissioners Office, and representatives of the Devon War Agricultural Executive committee, The Kingsbridge Rural District Council, the Admiralty and the Assistance Board.

The committee will give the closest consideration to all claims submitted in writing, and if you think that your case can receive adequate consideration in this way, you should submit it with supporting statements or evidence to the Principal Officer, Office of the Regional Commissioner, 19, Woodland Road, Bristol, 8, as soon as possible. If you would prefer to present your case orally to the committee, they will be sitting to consider claims at … on… and you are invited to appear before them when you will be asked to state your case and support it by such evidence as you may wish to produce. Will you please in any case let the Principal Officer know whether you wish to make any claim and, if so, whether you desire to appear before the committee. If you do so you should bring this letter with you in case you are stopped by the Police in connection with travel restrictions, which are now in force in certain areas.

Yours truly,
Hugh Elles
Regional Commissioner

CIVIL DEFENCE
OFFICE OF THE REGIONAL COMMISSIONER

Phone. No: Bristol 23346  
Telegrams: EMREGCOM, BRISTOL

South Western Regional Office,
19, Woodland Road,
BRISTOL, 8.
22nd April, 1944

Dear Sir or Madam,

A fund has been made available to the Regional Commissioner by the United States Army to help cases of distress arising out of the evacuation. This fund cannot be used for making any general addition to the compensation, which has been awarded. It is intended solely for the assistance of those who are in actual distress or have suffered a serious lowering of their standard of living, and financial loss will not in itself be sufficient to establish a claim. It is also a condition of the fund that it should not be applied to cases where help is forthcoming from other official sources. Therefore if you are eligible for a supplementary pension or a grant under the scheme for the prevention and relief of distress, you should apply to the Assistance Board and not for help from the fund.

The Regional Commissioner has appointed a committee to administer the fund, and invitations to appear before the committee have been sent to those whom there is reason to believe may be eligible for help. If you have not received such an invitation, but consider your case to come within the conditions set out above, you are invited to reply to the Principal Officer, Regional Commissioners Office, 19, Woodland Road, Bristol, 8, before May 5th, 1944 giving full particulars of the circumstances which entitled you to make a claim. You will then be given an opportunity to state your case to the committee, sitting at Kingsbridge, in the latter half of May.

To save yourself disappointment, you are asked not to apply unless you feel confident that your case comes clearly within the limits laid down. The Regional Commissioner recognises that there must be many cases of financial loss which do not come within these limits. But it has been found impossible to give the inhabitants of this area generally more favourable conditions than have been applied to many thousands of people elsewhere whose property has been requisitioned for purposes connected with the war.

I want to assure you, on behalf of the United States authorities as well as the regional commissioner, that they appreciate the sacrifice, which you have made. If you are in distress or if you feel your standard of living has definitely been lowered and you conscientiously feel that yours is a hardship case, you are invited to present it to this office for consideration by the committee.

Yours Truly
Principal Officer

Dear Sir
13th May, 1944

<u>S.W Evacuation Area: U.S Army Fund</u>.

The committee appointed by the Regional Commissioner has completed twelve days of work. Our experience has shown that perhaps too narrow a view has been taken by many as to the restrictive conditions set out in the letters from the regional Commissioners Office and that, nevertheless, cases of hardship do exist other than those already considered.

Before claims to the Fund available are closed, we should like to give you one further opportunity to present a case by personal appearance or letter if you desire to do so. The committee will sit for four additional days from 10am to 4pm on:–

Saturday, May 20th at the town Hall, Torquay.
Monday, May 22nd at the town Hall, Torquay.
Tuesday, May 23rd at the Manor House, Kingsbridge.
Wednesday, May 24th at the Rutter Library, 10 High Street, Totnes.

A form of reply is enclosed for you convenience and this should be addressed:–

The Principal Officer,
Regional Commissioners Office,
19, Woodland Road, Bristol,8.
Yours faithfully,

John E. Daw

Chairman of the committee

(Source: The National Archive File T 161/1168 – Compensation. Departments: Admiralty: Admiralty: Slapton evacuation scheme; compensation arrangements)

*Appendix B*

# The Compensation Scheme

A Scheme for the award of money for hardship cases of persons evacuated from the Slapton area.

1. The first step will be a preliminary assessment of the amount to meet hardship cases caused by the evacuation of the Slapton Sands Area for the use of the US Army in training manoeuvres. This will be made by representatives of the U.S Army and the Regional Commissioner, as a basis on which the U.S Army will decide the fund to be allotted.

The basis of this assessment will definitely be hardship and not loss. That is to say mere pecuniary loss will give no claim to payment from the fund unless it is accompanied by distress or by a material lowering of the standard of living.

2. All awards should be made by a committee sitting part of the time at Kingsbridge and part at Torquay.

This committee should consist of representatives of:–

The US Army.
The Regional commissioner.
Devon County Council.
Kingsbridge Rural District Council.
The Admiralty Lands Branch.
The Assistance Board.
The War Agricultural Executive Committee.

A representative of the South Hams Fellowship will be invited to be present but will not be a member of the committee and will have no vote.

3. All persons on the hardship list should be given a date on which to appeal personally before the committee. They will be informed in the notice given that they must appear in person with all the evidence needed to establish their case, but if they are unable owing to distance or for other sufficient reasons to be present and desire their case to be considered, they should forward a full statement of their case with full supporting evidence to the committee before the date fixed for the hearing of their case.

4. Notice will be served in the first place only upon those whose names are on the hardship list, but an advertisement will be inserted in the Western Morning News and other papers as desirable (preferably over a period of one week) informing persons concerned of the existence of the fund and committee, inviting with suitable safeguards all those who have not received notice to attend the committee to state their case in writing and announcing that those who do so will be given a date for appearance before the committee.

5. When the committee meets, it will know the total sum, which has been made available by the US Army. It will make provisional awards proportioned to the total fund available. When all cases have been dealt with, the provisional awards will be totalled, and will be diminished or increased by percentage, which will make the sum awarded equal to the fund available.

6. The basis of the awards must be hardship and not mere pecuniary loss, and no award will be made to a person who is eligible for supplementary pension or PRD but has failed to apply for it. It will be emphasised throughout that all awards are discretionary and are not made upon a basis of legal or quasi-legal right.

7. The fund made available by the US Army will be paid as a lump sum to the Regional Commissioner, and will be distributed by him in accordance with the awards of the committee. He will have the discretion whether to settle awards by a lump payment or by instalments.

8. After the conclusion of the proceedings copies of the final award will be furnished to the US Army.

(Source: The National Archive File T 161/1168 – Compensation. Departments: Admiralty: Admiralty: Slapton evacuation scheme; compensation arrangements)

# Posters Displayed Throughout the Area Announcing the News of the Evacuation

## Important Meetings

The area described below is to be REQUISITIONED urgently for military purposes, and must be cleared of its inhabitants by DECEMBER 20th 1943.

Arrangements have been made to help people in their moves to settle them elsewhere, and to assist them in the many problems with which they will be faced. To explain these arrangements

PUBLIC MEETINGS
Will be held as follows:

FRIDAY Nov.12th    11am East Allington Church
                      2.30pm Stokenham Church
Earl Fortescue, M.C., The Lord Lieutenant
In the Chair

SATURDAY Nov. 13th 11am Blackawton Church
                      2.30pm Slapton Village Hall
Sir John Daw, J.P., Chairman Devon County Council
In the Chair

These general meetings will be immediately followed by special meetings to discuss the problems of farmers, who are requested to remain behind for them.

# IMPORTANT MEETINGS

The area described below is to be REQUISITIONED urgently for military purposes, and must be cleared of its inhabitants by DECEMBER 20th, 1943.

Arrangements have been made to help the people in their moves, to settle them elsewhere, and to advise and assist them in the many problems with which they will be faced. To explain these arrangements

# PUBLIC MEETINGS

will be held as follows:

**FRIDAY Nov. 12th**

11 a.m.
## EAST ALLINGTON CHURCH

2-30 p.m.
## STOKENHAM CHURCH

**Earl Fortescue, M.C., The Lord Lieutenant**
in the Chair.

**SATURDAY Nov. 13th**

11 a.m.
## BLACKAWTON CHURCH

2-30 p.m.
## SLAPTON VILLAGE HALL

**Sir John Daw, J.P., Chairman Devon County Council**
in the Chair.

These general meetings will be immediately followed by special meetings to discuss the problems of farmers, who are requested to remain behind for them.

IT IS VITALLY IMPORTANT to every householder that he should arrange to attend whichever of these meetings is nearest to his home, and where necessary employers of labour are requested to give their work-people time off for this purpose.

# THE AREA AFFECTED

ALL LAND AND BUILDINGS lying within the line from the sea at the east end of Blackpool Bay in Stoke Fleming parish to Bowden; thence northward along the road to the Sportsman's Arms; thence west along the Dittisham-Halwell road to the cross-roads ¼-mile east of Halwell village; from this cross-road along the Kingsbridge road to the Woodleigh-Buckland cross-roads; thence along the road Buckland, Frogmore, Chillington, Beeson and Beesands to the sea, but excluding the villages of Frogmore, Beeson and Beesands. The roads forming the boundary are outside the area.

The parishes involved are the whole, or almost the whole, of Blackawton, East Allington, Sherford, Slapton and Strete, most of Stokenham, and parts of Stoke Fleming, Buckland-tout-Saints and Halwell.

IT IS VITALLY IMPORTANT to every householder that he should arrange to attend whichever of these meetings is nearest to his home, and where necessary employers of labour are requested to give their work people time off for this purpose.

## THE AREA AFFECTED

ALL LAND AND BUILDINGS within the line from the sea at the end of Blackpool Bay in Stoke Fleming parish to Bowden; thence northward along the road to the Sportsman's Arms; thence west along the Dittisham-Halwell road the crossroads ¼ mile east of Halwell village; from this crossroads along the Kingsbridge road to Woodleigh-Buckland crossroads; thence along the road Buckland, Frogmore, Chillington, Beeson and Beesands to the sea but excluding the villages of Frogmore, Beeson and Beesands. The roads forming the boundary are outside the area. The parishes involved are the whole or almost the whole of Blackawton, East Allington, Sherford, Slapton, and Strete, most of Stokenham and parts of Stoke Fleming, Buckland-tout-Saints and Halwell.

*Appendix D*

# The Evacuation Notice Sent to
# All Those in the Area

**THIS GIVES YOU IMPORTANT INFORMATION AND ADVICE. PLEASE READ IT CAREFULLY**

**FIRST OF ALL** fill in as fully as you can the enquiry form you will find with these papers. There is a space provided for your special problems; use it and write on the back if you have not room in front. A WVS representative will come to collect the form after 4 days, and will, if you ask, help you to fill it in. If you come to the Information Centre before the form has been collected, bring it with you.

**INFORMATION CENTRES** will be set up at Stokenham (for the parishes of Stokenham, Slapton, Sherford and Buckland-tout-Saints) and at Blackawton (for the parishes of Blackawton, East Allington, Woodleigh, Halwell, Stoke Fleming and Strete). They will be open daily from 9.30am to 6.00pm. You will find there officers, who will be able to advise and help you, whatever the difficulty may be. Do not hesitate to make the fullest use of your Centre. Take your little worries there, as well as your big ones. But you must go to the Centre to which the Parish in which you live has been allotted. Whether you are going to move yourself, or whether you are looking for us to move you, fix as early a date for your departure as you can. Of course, you would like to stay in your home until the last possible day. But those who go first are going to get the best accommodation and the best transport, so don't wait for the rush, the hurry and the discomfort of the last few days.

**HOW YOU CAN BE HELPED**
1. COMPENSATION
On all questions concerning compensation about which you are not clear you should consult the Admiralty. They have offices at both Information

Centres, and wherever possible an Officer will visit you and give you any explanations you require.

## 2. ACCOMMODATION

You should endeavour at once to find other accommodation for yourself and family outside the area (of which the boundaries are given at the end of this note). If you find it impossible to make your own arrangements in this way, the Local Authority will find you accommodation outside the area, but they can give no guarantee of an unfurnished house or rooms and it is almost certain that compulsory billeting in an occupied house will be necessary. If you have special difficulties due to your being unable to find accommodation suitable for invalids, expectant mothers, old and infirm people, you should say so when filling in your form and should consult the Information Centre as well.

## 3. BILLETING

If you are provided with accommodation for yourself and family in an occupied house, whether by your own arrangement or by the authorities, the householder will be entitled to a billeting allowance at the rate of 5/- per week for each adult and 3/- per week for each child under the age of 14. This billeting allowance will be payable for TWO WEEKS without recovery but if the payment of the allowance is continued beyond two weeks, recovery will be made from you up to the full amount of the allowance, according to your financial circumstances.

If you are making your own arrangements to share accommodation with relatives, friends or other family outside the area, you should apply to the Information Centre for the issue of a certificate authorising the payment of billeting allowance.

## 4. TRANSPORT

The reasonable cost of all necessary journeys will be paid to you, and owners of vehicles of any kind may use them freely for the removal from the area of their families, furniture and effects or those of their neighbours. If you have a motor vehicle which is unlicensed, you can obtain from the Information Centre a special certificate which will enable you to use it for the above purposes within an area for a period which will be entered in the certificate. You may also use your private car to go to the Information Centre, or to make reasonable journeys outside the area in connection with accommodation, storage or employment.

In all these cases you can obtain petrol coupons from the Information Centre. Cars can also be made available by the Information Centre to take you on necessary journeys. During the first fortnight you will be able to make your own arrangements for the removal of your furniture with a furniture remover or other carrier (of which the reasonable cost will be repaid to you). In this way you will be able to arrange your move to suit your own convenience. After this fortnight all transport is likely to be controlled, and will then only be obtainable through the Information Centres. All applications to the Centres should give full details of the time and place at which transport is required, the load (eg contents of a four-roomed cottage) and the destinations. Transport will then be provided according to a planned programme designed to secure speed and economy.

## 5. STORAGE
If you are going to store your furniture you should make arrangements with a repository outside the area. If you cannot find storage room there, come to the Information Centre, and arrangements will be made for you.

## 6. FARMERS
Every help will be given you by the War Agricultural Executive committee at Blackawton including assistance in the removal or disposal of your stock and of your cattle feed and other farm produce, and in making arrangements to enable you to complete your threshing and lifting your roots.

## 7. FARM WORKERS
If you work on a farm, or do any other work actually connected with farming at Blackawton, you should consult the representative of the War Agricultural Executive committee who will find you work. You should not go in search of work yourself, but if you do find a new farm post of your own you should tell the War Agricultural Executive committee at once.

## 8. OTHER PERSONS SEEKING EMPLOYMENT
Should consult the representative of the Ministry of Labour at the Information Centre.

## 9. SHOPKEEPERS
A representative of the Ministry of Food or the Board of Trade will visit you as soon as possible, and will make arrangements for the removal and disposal of your stocks. If you keep a food shop and wish to move at an early date (i.e. before your customers have gone) you should at once inform the Food Executive Officer, Kingsbridge Rural District, of your intention.

## 10. RATION BOOKS AND IDENTITY CARDS
As you will be changing your address it will be necessary in due course to amend the particulars on your ration book and identity card. You should enquire at your local food office or at your Information Centre how you should proceed.

## 11. PUBLICANS
Your License will not be extinguished by the closing of your houses. It will come into force again on your return.

## 12. EDUCATION
Elementary school children will attend school at the places to which they move. The parents of children attending secondary schools should inform the Information Centre. Individual arrangements will be made to enable them to continue their studies.

## 13. PENSIONS AND ASSISTANCE
Give in your form particulars of pensions or any form of monetary aid received by any member of your household. Representatives of the Assistance Board will visit all persons in receipt of supplementary pensions and will deal with any case in which urgent financial assistance is required. Arrangements will be made for the prompt payment of Old Age Pensions at the post office of the place to which the pensioner has transferred.

## 14. POST OFFICE SERVICES

The post office will make arrangements for the prompt forwarding of letters and will deliver at your house a re-direction card to be filled up. At the same time, you should be careful to notify your change of address to members of your family, especially to those who are serving in the Forces.

## 15. PROFITEERING

Any attempt to charge you unfair rent, or to profiteer on transport or storage charges, should be reported at once to the Information Centre, and in the case of rent, to the Local Authority concerned.

*Appendix E*

# List of Major Exercises

| Date | Code name | Exercise details | Troops taking part | Exercise Air Force allotted |
|---|---|---|---|---|
| 27 Dec 43–4 Jan 44 | DUCK 1 | Regimental Combat Team Landing | 29th Inf Div, built around the 175th Inf Regt, units of the 1st Eng Sp Brig, and various attachments including an IX Air Force beach party and a headquarters group of V Corps | |
| 9 Feb–14 Feb 1944 | DUCK 2 | Regimental Combat Team Landing | 116th Regimental Landing Team of the 29th Div, and the 1st Bn of the 531st Engineer Shore Regiment, together with other 1st Brigade elements and attached V Corps units | |
| 29 Feb 1944 | DUCK 3 | Regimental Combat Team Landing | 115th Regimental Landing Team of the 29th Div and 1st Brigade elements | |
| 9–10 March | FOX | Regimental Combat Team Landing – rehearsal | 16th RCT of the 1st Inf Div and the 116th RCT of the 29th Inf Div, working under control of 1st Inf Div headquarters which in turn was under a headquarters group from V Corps | |
| 27–31 March 30 Mar–D-Day 31 Mar–Spare Day | BEAVER | Full-scale Divisional assault | VII (US) Corps, 11 Amph Force Force 'U' and 4 US Division | 4 Sqdns light or medium bombers 6 Sqdn fighter bombers, 9 Sqdn fighters, 1 Flt Fighter Recce, All from Allied TAF's HQ ship |

| Date | Code name | Exercise details | Troops taking part | Exercise Air Force allotted |
| --- | --- | --- | --- | --- |
| 1–11 April | CARGOV | To perform far shore duties in support of a task force (assumed); to develop beach and dump facilities including road construction | 6th Engr Special Brigade | |
| 12–16 April | TROUSERS | Full-scale divisional assault landing on two brigade fronts and reserve brigade follow through. HQ ships to participate (sea passage of 100 miles) | 3 Cdn Div Force 'J' and 3 Cdn Div | 6 Sqdns light or medium bombers (smoke laying a/c to be provided from light bombers) 6 Sqdn fighter bombers, 18 Sqdn fighters, 1 Flt Fighter Recce, All from Allied TAF's HQ Ship |
| 26–28 April | TIGER | Rehearsal | VII US Corps Force 'U' 4 (US) Division | 8 Sqdns light or medium bombers (smoke laying a/c to be provided from light bombers) 8 Sqdn fighter bombers, 12 Sqdn fighters, 1 Flt Fighter Recce, All from Allied TAF's HQ Ship |
| 3 May | FABIUS I | Rehearsal | Force 'O' elements of the 1st US Infantry Division, the 29th US Infantry Division, the Provisional Engineer Special Brigade Group, and attached units, which were to assault Omaha Beach under the command of V Corps | Full fighter cover with additional allotments |

# Glossary

AAA Awpns Bn – Anti-aircraft artillery (automatic weapons) battalion

AA – Anti-aircraft

AC2 – Aircraftsman second class

ADC – Aide-de-camp

AM Car Co – Armoured Car Company

ANXCF – Allied Naval Commander-in-Chief Expeditionary Force

APA – Attack transport

ATASC – Assault training area selection committee

AT – Anti-tank

AVRE – Armoured vehicle Royal engineers

Blinds – high explosive munitions that fail to detonate after being fired

Bn – Battalion

Btry – Battery (artillery gun battery)

CML Bn (Mtz) – Chemical Battalion Motorised

Co – Company

CoS – Chief of staff

COSSAC – Chief of Staff to Supreme Allied Commander

DD – Duplex Drive (amphibious tank)

Det – Detachment

Div – Division

DUKW – A six wheeled amphibious truck

GOC – General Officer commanding

Eng – Engineer

Eng Gp – Engineer Group

Engr Topo Co – Engineer topographical company

Eng Sp Brig – Engineer Special Brigade

ETO – European theatre of operations

ETOUSA – European Theater of Operations United States Army

FA – Field Artillery

FA Brig – Field Artillery Brigade

Fg Off – Flying Officer

FOB – Forward Observer

Hards – Embarkation slipways

HMT – Her Majesty's Transport

HQ – Headquarters

K-rations – US Army 1 man combat rations

LBV – Landing barge vehicle

LCA(HR) – Landing Craft Assault – Hedgerow

LCI – Landing Craft Infantry

LCI(L) – Landing Craft infantry – large
LCM – Landing craft mechanised
LCG – Landing Craft gun
LCT(A) – Landing Craft Tank – Armoured
LCT – Landing Craft Tank
LCT(R) – Landing Craft Rocket
LCVP – Landing Craft vehicle and personnel
LMG – Light machine gun
LSI – Landing ship infantry
LSI(H) – Landing ship infantry heavy
LSH – Landing ship headquarters
LSI(L) – Landing ship infantry large
LST – Landing ship Tank
MOD – UK Ministry of Defence
MOI – Ministry of Information
MP – Military Police
Neptune – the assault phase of Operation Overlord
NCO – Non-commissioned officer
PIR – Parachute Infantry Regiment
PM – Prime Minister
PRD – Prevention of Distress
Pvt – Private
PX – The Army & Air Force Post Exchange
QM – Quarter Master
QM TRK Regt – Quartermaster Truck Regiment
RCT – Regimental Combat team
RDC – Rural District council
SA – Small arms
SHAEF – Supreme headquarter allied expeditionary force
Sig Bn – Signal Battalion
Sommerfeld Track – A lightweight wire mesh type of prefabricated track
SOS – Service of Supply
SP – Self-propelled
Stick – Airborne assault collective term for a group of paratroopers as loaded on an aircraft.
TD – Tank Destroyer
WT – Wireless Telegraphy
WVS – Women's Voluntary Service
USMC – United States Marine Corps
RA – Royal Artillery
Pierced steel planking – Lightweight prefabricated track constructed of pressed steel plates that
    can be linked together.
TNT – Trinitrotoluene – explosive

# Notes

## Chapter 1

1. Renney Battery – located on the eastern side of Plymouth Sound. The principle battery for the Coast Artillery School at Plymouth until closed in 1956.
2. Lovering, Tristan, *Amphibious Assault: Manoeuvre from the Sea*. Seafarer books (2007)
3. *Ibid.*
4. *Ibid.*
5. *Ibid.*
6. The 'Battle of the Barges' – during July 1940, the Germans began assembling hundreds of barges in the French and Dutch coastal ports in preparation for the invasion of Britain. Bomber Command repeatedly attacked these ports destroying invasion barges whilst also attacking enemy air bases, fuel supplies and aircraft. More RAF bomber crew members were killed during the period of the Battle of Britain than fighter pilots.
7. Lovering, *op.cit.*
8. http://www.naval-history.net/WW2CampaignsItaly.htm – CAMPAIGN SUMMARIES OF WORLD WAR 2 ITALY and the ITALIAN CAMPAIGN, including Sicily, Salerno & Anzio Landings 1943–1945
9. Lovering, *op.cit.*
10. Official report, Hansard, Thursday, October 4, 2012
11. Lovering, *op.cit.*
12. http://www.nps.gov/history/history/online_books/npswapa/extcontent/usmc/pcn-190-003120-00/sec8.htm (Across the Reef: The Marine Assault of Tarawa by Colonel Joseph H. Alexander, USMC (Ret))
13. Lovering, *op.cit.*

## Chapter 2

1. The *Lancashire* was built by Harland & Wolff in Belfast in 1917. She initially sailed under the Liner Requisition Scheme as a troopship and it was not until 1920 that she was released to the Bibby Line and placed on the Birkenhead – Rangoon service. In 1930 Cammell Laird at Birkenhead converted the *Lancashire* into a full-time troopship. After extensive service during the Second World War, the *Lancashire* was reconditioned by Harland & Wolff at Govan in 1946 and continued as a troopship, voyaging to Cyprus, India and the Far East, she was broken up at Barrow-in-Furness in 1956. The ship acted as commodore ship for Juno Beach during the D-Day landings.
2. SS *Clan MacAlister* – British Cargo Steamer of 6,787 tons built in 1930 by Greenock Dockyard Company, Greenock for the Clan Line Steamers Ltd, Glasgow. On the 29th May 1940 she was sunk by a German air raid whilst off Dunkirk.
3. HMS *Sheffield* was one of the Southampton Town class cruisers of the Royal Navy during the Second World War. She took part in actions against several major German warships including the *Bismarck* and the *Tirpitz*. She survived the war and was scrapped at Faslane in 1967.

4. HMS *Southampton* – Town class Light Cruiser. Launched 10 March 1936 sunk off Malta 11 January 1941.
5. HMS *Courageous* was launched on 5 February 1916 as battlecruiser and converted to an aircraft carrier in 1924. She was sunk by the German submarine U–29 in September 1939.
6. HMS *Revenge*. Revenge class battleship launched 29 May 1915, scrapped Inverkeithing 1948.
7. 3rd Infantry division units taking place in the exercise:
   2nd Battalion, The Middlesex Regiment (Duke of Cambridge's Own) based at New Barracks, Gosport
   9th Infantry Brigade
   2nd Battalion, The Lincolnshire Regiment, based at Portsmouth
   1st Battalion, The Kings Own Scottish Borderers, based at Portsmouth
   8th Infantry Brigade
   2nd Battalion, The East Yorkshire Regiment (The Duke of York's Own) based at Plymouth
   2nd Battalion, The Gloucestershire Regiment based at Plymouth
8. The same Montgomery who would become Field Marshal Bernard Law Montgomery, 1st Viscount Montgomery of Alamein, KG GCB DSO PC. Montgomery was promoted to temporary Brigadier on 5 August 1937.
9. *Western Morning News* – article 'On the other side', Thursday 7 July 1938.
10. *Ibid.*
11. *Ibid.*
12. *Ibid.*
13. DEFE 2/709 Manual of Combined Operations

**Chapter 3**
1. WO 219/932 Procurement and use of training areas and ranges in UK

**Chapter 4**
War diaries referred to:
70th Brigade – WO 167/385 01 May 1940 – 31 May 1940
70th Brigade – WO 176/304 – 01 August 1940 – 31 December 1941
11 DLI – WO 167/732 01 April 1940 – 30 June 1940
11 DLI – WO 176/332 01 July 1940 – 31 December 1941

1. Admiralty scaffolding, also known as Obstacle Z1, or sometimes simply given as beach scaffolding or anti-tank scaffolding, was a British design of anti-tank and anti-boat obstacle made of tubular steel.
2. http://www.iwm.org.uk/collections/item/object/80008976 (IWM Interview with Kenneth Johnstone, 11th Battalion Durham Light Infantry)
3. This was a flame-thrower type weapon constructed of a simple arrangement of perforated steel pipes, one to two inches in diameter and drilled with holes at angles. The perforated pipes were connected to larger pipes that led to a tank of fuel in a raised position. The fuel mixture was 25% petrol and 75% gas-oil. To trigger the weapon a valve was opened and the fuel ignited creating an inferno.
4. The assumption is that this was a World War One vintage British SBML (smooth bore muzzle-loading) 6-inch mortar. This rather simple and crude weapon fired bombs weighing 60lbs filled with high explosive and fin-stabilised, both primer and propellant charge being accommodated in the fins. Firing was by fixed striker in the breech.
5. Appendix from War Diary Appendix A1 – issued 3rd September 1940 – Air Spray Demonstration – Secret. The briefing paper describes the purpose of the demonstration,

namely: to show what a low–altitude Spray Attack looks like; to practise the warnings given for this type of attack; to practise protective measures on the move.

    Commanders were expected to read the relevant paragraphs from the pamphlets on Protection against Gas and Air Raids. The dress to be worn, and the equipment to be carried were to be normal, with the inclusion of anti-gas eye shields and detectors. Transport arrangements and timings were set out. The venue was to be Slapton Sands. Road blocks would be in place to prevent traffic or civilians reaching the area. Anti-aircraft protection was to be mounted using Bren guns.

6. Personal recollection: http://www.newmp.org.uk/70brigade/index.php/70th_Infantry_Brigade_War_Diary_June_1940
7. http://www.goldendays.org.uk/reg-hannaford-2/ (Recording made by Blackawton & Strete History (BASH) Group for the AONB in 2010)
8. Ramsey, Winston G., *The Blitz Then and Now*, *Vol. 2* (After the Battle) 1988
9. Rose-Price, Robin and Parnell, Jean, *The Land we Left Behind*, Orchard Publications
10. Goss, Chris with Peter Cornwell and Bernd Rauchbach, *Luftwaffe Fighter Bombers Over Britain*, Crecy Publishing
11. Commonwealth War Graves Commission: http://www.cwgc.org/find-war-dead.aspx
12. Goss, Chris, *op.cit.*
13. http://www.goldendays.org.uk/pam-wills/
14. http://www.goldendays.org.uk/ken-parnell/
15. http://www.aircrewremembrancesociety.co.uk/styled-15/styled-20/styled-68/index.html
16. The Air Forces Memorial at Runnymede commemorates by name over 20,000 airmen who were lost in the Second World War during operations from bases in the United Kingdom and North and Western Europe, and who have no known graves. They served in bomber, fighter, coastal, transport, flying training and maintenance commands, and came from all parts of the Commonwealth. Some were from countries in continental Europe which had been overrun but whose airmen continued to fight in the ranks of the Royal Air Force. http://www.cwgc.org/find-a-cemetery/cemetery/109600/RUNNYMEDE%20MEMORIAL

## Chapter 5

1. COSSAC (Chief of Staff to Supreme Allied Commander). The aim of COSSAC was defined as: Our object is to defeat the German fighting forces in northwest Europe. To this end the Combined Chiefs of Staff will endeavour to assemble the strongest possible forces (subject to prior commitments in other theatres) in constant readiness to re-enter the continent if German resistance is weakened to the required extent in 1943. In the meantime the Combined Chiefs of Staff must be prepared to order such limited operations as may be practicable with the forces and material available.
2. The US Army Assault Training Centre at Woolacombe in North Devon was established on 1st September 1943 to teach and train American infantry the tactics of amphibious assault.
3. ADM 116/5080 Operation 'Overlord': amphibious assault training area.
4. Force O would comprise elements of the US V Corps and be responsible for the assault of Omaha Beach.
5. Whilst these dimensions were generous, it was noted that they would still not permit the firing of anti-tank guns against dummy targets except on a very restricted scale, and firing from tanks during the assault phase would also have to be restricted.
    The ranges of some of the support weapons that would be utilised during the assault training are listed below:
LCT (A) HE (95mm): 6,000 yards
LCT (R): 4,000 yards

LCA(HR): 400 yards

SP 105mm from LCT: 13,000 yards

(WO 205/1091 Assault training areas: Southern Command)

6. WO 205/1091 Assault training areas: Southern Command

7. Norman Daniel 'Dutch' Cota, Sr. (1893–1971). As a Brigadier General he served as the United States adviser to the Combined Operations Division of the European Theatre of Operations. As an advisor and Assistant Division commander of the 29th Infantry Division, he helped to observe and supervise in the training of landing operations. He was heavily involved in the planning and execution of the invasion of France, codenamed Operation Neptune, and the subsequent Battle of Normandy. Cota landed with a part of the 116th Infantry Regiment of the 29th Division, in the second wave, approximately one hour after H-Hour, on the Omaha sector known as Dog White, his boat coming under heavy machine gun fire as well as mortar and light artillery fire. Cota was one of the highest ranking officers on the beach that day. He is famous for personally directing the attack, motivating the shell-shocked, pinned-down survivors into action, and opening one of the first vehicle exits off the beach. A famous quote attributed to him that day was, 'Gentlemen, we are being killed on the beaches. Let us go inland and be killed.'

8. ETOUSA – European Theater of Operations United States Army. HQ
ETOUSA was established in London 8 June 1942, succeeding Headquarters US Army in the British Isles (HQ USABI) until the establishment of Supreme Headquarters Allied Expeditionary Force (SHAEF) on 13 February 1944. HQ ETOUSA participated in operational planning for Allied invasion of western Europe; performed administrative and service functions for US Army troops, equipment and facilities in UK and Iceland, 1942–45; North Africa, November 1942–February 1943; and Western Europe, 6 June 1944–1 July 1945.

9. The other areas selected were:
Gower Peninsula, Glamorgan – required for full assault training, firing and manoeuvring throughout the area. Required for use by 15 December 1943

Tarbet Peninsula, Argyll and Bute – full assault training, firing and manoeuvring throughout the area. Required for use by 1 December 1943

Culbin Sands, Inverness-shire. Required for assault landings, with firing by sea-borne support only. Required by 1 December 1943

Burghead Bay, Morayshire. Required for full assault training, firing manoeuvring throughout the area. Required by 1 December 1943

(ADM 116/5080 Operation 'Overlord': amphibious assault training area)

10. Full list of those attending:
The Rt. Hon. C.R. Attlee MP (Chairman)

First Lord of the Admiralty the Rt. Hon. A.V. Alexander

The Rt. Hon. Thomas Johnston MP, Secretary of State for Scotland

The Rt. Hon. R.S. Hudson MP, Minister of Agriculture and Fisheries

Lord Sherwood, Parliamentary under-secretary for Air

Sir Edward Bridges, Secretary to the War Cabinet

Rear Admiral G.E. Creasy, COSSAC

Captain A.J.L. Phillips RN, Director of Local Defence, Admiralty

The Rt. Hon. Sir James Grigg MP, Secretary of State for War

The Rt. Hon. Ernest Brown MP, Minister of Health

Captain the Rt. Hon. H.F.C. Crookshank MP, Postmaster-General

Lieut-General A.E. Nye, Vice-Chief of the Imperial General Staff

Sir Findalter Stuart, Home Defence Executive
Air Commodore W.E. Yool, Director of Organisation, Air Ministry
Colonel Matthews, War Office
MR. S. Hoare, Home Office
(WO 219/932 Procurement and use of training areas and ranges in UK)

**Appendix to Chapter 5**
ADM 116/5080 Operation 'Overlord': amphibious assault training area,
Reconnaissance for training areas

Combined reconnaissance of Slapton Sands, Bigbury Bay, Veryan Bay and St Austell Bay were carried out on 3 and 4 August 1943 by:-

Captain W.B Hynes. RN
Lieutenant Colonel R.O. Bare, USMC
Major J.I. Littlewood RA
Mr. S.G. Fowler, Surveyor of Lands, Devonport, for Dartmouth Area
Mr. A.C. Morgan, representing surveyor of Lands, Devonport for Cornwall.
Report:
Start Bay – Blackpool Bay
The Frontage is 10,000 yards
The required depth of 5,000–6,000 yards is nowhere practicable owing to:-
Unsuitability of hinterland for vehicle deployment;
Limited exits from beaches;
Importance of agricultural interests affected;
Population of the area affected which would exceed 1,500;
The main road, which runs in close proximity to the coast from Stoke Fleming 290700 to Torcross 250638;
There are beaches:
I) Blackpool Bay: 600 yards
II) Slapton Sands: northern section from 68 grid line to road junction 262673: 800 yards
III) Slapton Sands: southern section from hotel 257659 to 252644: 1800 yards
IV) Bee Sands from Sunnydale 249631 to 248634: 600 yards
V) Hall Sands from Tinsey Head 247614 to Greenstraight 245608 to 700 yards

Suitability of beaches:
Blackpool: the whole length is unusable at all states of tide, but is subject to interference from easterly weather. One exit from beach to Main Road.
Slapton Sands (north): the whole length is usable at all states of the tide, subject to weather. There is one exit for vehicles to the main road at the southern extremity.
Slapton Sands (south): the whole length is usable at all states of the tides, subject to weather. There are exits for vehicles to main road over the full length of the beach, but owing to the Ley, access to the hinterland is limited to road exits at north end, centre and south end of the Ley.
Beesands: the whole length is usable at all states of the tide, subject to weather. There is one exit for vehicles at the southern extremity.
Hallsands: the whole length is usable at all stages of the tide, subject to weather. There is one exit for vehicles at the southern extremity.

The beach at Blackpool is mainly sand but on the remainder of the beach it is formed of loose shingle with gradients up to 1 in 4 which constantly changes as a result of winds and tides. This type of beach presents a serious obstruction to the passage of both wheeled and tracked vehicles. It would be necessary to lay roadways on the occasion of each exercise.

The approaches to beaches I, II, and III are easy. The direct approach to beach IV is across Skerries Bank at a distance of two miles. The direct approach to beach V is definitely obstructed by the Skerries Bank.

The whole front is covered by a convoy route which is swept at frequent intervals. No special minesweeping is considered necessary.

There are landmines at various points which would require lifting. It is suggested that other beach obstacles be left for training purposes.

Recommendations:

The area as a whole is not considered suitable and is not recommended for the purpose outlined in Admiralty letter of 7 July 1943.

It is considered that all the beaches detailed in paragraph 3 can be usefully employed for landing exercises NOT involving the firing of live ammunition and NOT involving the subsequent deployment of vehicles.

With reference to the commander-in-chief, Portsmouth's 251410/B July 1943, para 4, it would be possible to clear an area behind beaches III and IV to a depth of 500 yards to permit the firing of rockets and smoke mortars, observing, however, that the great majority of projectiles will fall in water or marsh.

Bigbury Bay:

The area from Bantham to Ringmore was also inspected but fails to provide facilities required. The beaches at Bantham, Bigbury and Challaborough are very open to the southwest, but can usefully be used for practise without live ammunition for naval training when weather permits.

**Chapter 6**

1. ADM 1/15002 Compensation (9): compensation arrangements for farmers in Slapton Sands area; additional compensation refused on grounds of 1939 Act of Parliament
2. T 161/1168 Compensation: Departments: Admiralty: Admiralty: Slapton evacuation scheme; compensation arrangements
3. WO 219/932 Procurement and use of training areas and ranges in UK
4. Lieutenant General Sir Hugh Jamieson Elles KCB KCMG KCVO DSO (1880-1945) served in the Second Boer War. He was instrumental in helping set up the use of tanks with the British Army and was the first commander of the newly formed Tank Corps during the First World War. In 1917 he personally led 350 tanks into battle at Cambrai in a Mark IV tank called Hilda. He is also credited with the design of the Corps flag of brown, red and green silk. After the war, he commanded the Tank Corps Training Centre at Bovington and later served as Inspector of Tank Corps at the War Office. During his army career he also commanded an Infantry Brigade, served as Director of Military Training, and as a Divisional commander. In April 1934 he was appointed Master-General of the Ordnance in the rank of Lieutenant General. He retired in 1938 and in the early years of the Second World War was chief of Civil Defence operational staff (June 1940). Later he was appointed South West Regional Commissioner based in Bristol and would have taken regional command of the resistance in the event of a German invasion and occupation of Britain.
5. Albert Victor Alexander, 1st Earl Alexander of Hillsborough KG CH PC (1885–1965) was a British Labour Co-operative politician. He was three times First Lord of the Admiralty,

including during the Second World War, and then Minister of Defence in the Labour government led by Clement Attlee in 1945.

6. ADM 1/15002 – Compensation (9): Compensation arrangements for farmers in Slapton Sands area; additional compensation refused on grounds of 1939 Act of Parliament
7. ADM 1/15002, *ibid.*
8. ADM 1/15002, *ibid.*
9. Brigadier Sir Ralph Herbert Rayner MBE (1897–1977) was a Conservative Party politician. Rayner was commissioned into the Duke of Wellington's Regiment in which he served as a signals officer. He was seconded to the Royal Flying Corps in 1916. During the First World War he served on the Western Front and India. He was seconded to the Indian Army in 1917 and served in the Third Afghan War. He transferred to the Royal Corps of Signals in the 1920s. Between 1928 and 1930 he was ADC to the Marquis of Willingdon, Governor General of Canada. He was promoted Captain in 1916, Major in 1919, and retired in 1933. He then entered politics and was MP for Totnes from 1935 to 1955. He rejoined the Army during the Second World War and reached the rank of Brigadier. He was knighted in 1956 and became High Sheriff of Devon in 1958.
10. ADM 1/17083 – Compensation (9): Financial aid from the American Red Cross for hardship cases amongst those affected by Slapton Sands requisition order
11. T 161/1168 Compensation: Departments: Admiralty: Admiralty: Slapton evacuation scheme; compensation arrangements
12. *Ibid.*
13. ADM 1/15002 Buildings and land (other than admiralty office and dockyards) (13): Compensation arrangements for farmers in Slapton Sands area; additional compensation refused on grounds of 1939 Act of Parliament
14. http://hansard.millbanksystems.com/commons/1943/dec/08/evacuation-area-south-west-england#S5CV0395P0_19431208_HOC_37 (Evacuation Area, South-West England (Ameliorative Measures) 8 *December 1943)*

## Chapter 7
1. T 161/1168 Compensation. Departments: Admiralty: Admiralty: Slapton evacuation scheme; compensation arrangements
2. To give these figures some context, the average annual wage in the UK in 1943 was approximately £355 per annum, making an average weekly wage of approximately £6 16/-. To put this in modern day terms, the average UK wage in 2012 was £26,500, producing an average weekly wage of £509.61. Therefore the weekly compensation payments in 1943 of £3 equate to approximately £250 per week.
3. T 161/1168, *ibid.*
4. General Edward C. Betts (1890–1946) was Judge Advocate European Theatre of Operations from 1942–6. Transferring from the infantry to the Judge Advocate General's Corps in 1929, he rose through the ranks to claim a professorship of law at the United States Military Academy at West Point in 1938. In the wake of the attack on Pearl Harbor, he was promoted to full colonel and named Judge Advocate, Headquarters, European Theatre of Operations, where he served as legal advisor to General Dwight D. Eisenhower. He rose to the rank of Brigadier General. His death from a sudden heart attack, at Frankfurt, Germany, on May 6, 1946, ended the preparations he was making for the trials of German war criminals at Nuremberg.
5. T 161/1168, *ibid.*
6. For his work with the Slapton evacuation claims, Major Rives received a Bronze Star Decoration. Bronze Star Citation:

To: Edwin E. Rives, Major A.G.D., 405 N.W. Greenway, Greensboro, NC.

For: Meritorious services in connection with military operations as a Special Commissioner representing the Theater Commander, 22 March 1944 to 11 June 1944. To facilitate the training of United States combat troops in the United Kingdom, it was necessary and imperative that large battle training areas be requisitioned through the medium of British War Office and Admiralty authorities. Upon the request of the United States Ambassador a large area of land in Southwestern England, including several towns and 30,000 acres of farm land, known as Slapton Sands, was acquired. In view of the proposed firing with live ammunition of all calibers it was necessary that many hundred local inhabitants be completely evacuated. The evictees were subjected to certain hardships and losses in their business and property for which they could not be compensated by either the British authorities or the United States Army through normal legal process under the then existing relief or claims regulations. The Theater Commander, as a matter of policy for the furtherance of Anglo–American goodwill, charged Major Rives with the delicate and difficult duty of effecting special compensation in the hardship cases, within the limits of propriety and without the benefits of, or the power to create, precedent. In order to carry out this responsibility Major Rives obtained the cooperation and consent of the British War Office, the Admiralty, the Treasurer Solicitor and the Chancellor of the Exchequer to this project. With extreme diplomacy in avoiding all misunderstanding Major Rives formed a group of influential officials known as the Regional Commissioner's Committee and carried out his mission of goodwill compensation payments with great tact, justice, and fair dealing. It was of paramount importance that the hundreds of cases be examined, handled, and paid with a high degree of discretion that there be no admission of liability and that no precedent be created to the possible detriment of the United States. By his action and services Major Rives contributed immeasurably to the furtherance of the Allied war effort and to Anglo–American relations.

Major Rives was born in Winston-Salem, NC, and attended the University of North Carolina where he received his LL.B in 1922. He engaged in the general practise of law in Greensboro NC from 1922 to 1929. From 1929 to 1943 he was judge of the Municipal County Court, Greensboro NC. He was appointed Captain in the Army of the United States and ordered to active duty in April 1943.

### Chapter 8

1. HO 186/1229 Operation Overlord, Slapton battle area map and regulations.
2. http://www.goldendays.org.uk/eddie-bowles/ (recording made by Blackawton & Strete History (BASH) Group for the AONB in 2010)
3. *Western Morning News* Thursday, 11 November 1943
4. ADM 1/17026 Admiralty (5): Safeguarding valuable property in the Slapton Sands assault training area
5. *ibid.*

### Chapter 9

1. WO 205/977 Report of a conference on landing assaults held at HQ Assault Training Centre, European Theatre of Operations, US Army: Part I
2. *Ibid.*
3. *Ibid.*

### Chapter 10

1. Embarkation hards were built by the Admiralty as part of Operation Overlord to load landing vessels in preparation for D-Day and the invasion of occupied Europe. A total of sixty-eight

individual hards were constructed between 1942 and 1944 across the southern coast of England in every county between Suffolk and Cornwall. There were two types of embarkation hards: LCT hards for landing crafts for troops, and LST hards for landing ships carrying tanks. A standard hard consisted of a rectangular concrete apron that sloped down into the water, which was equipped with steel framed mooring points (known as dolphins) to moor the vessels during loading. Hard sites included access roads to link the hards to public highways, approach roads to accommodate the concentrated heavy traffic, and transit areas for marshalling troops, vehicles and equipment. Accommodation and ancillary buildings at hard sites would include offices for embarkation staff, a central control room, a workshop for maintenance crew, stores, a watch hut, and a latrine. Sites were also fitted with fuel, lighting and utilities.

2. Yung, Christopher, *Gators of Neptune: Naval Amphibious Planning for the Normandy Invasion*, Naval Institute Press (2006)
3. Captain Harry C. Butcher USNR, *My Three Years with Eisenhower*, Simon and Schuster, New York, 1946, pages 527–9.
4. *Ibid.*

**General References for Chapter 10**
This chapter references a number of histories and original documentation. These sources are listed here:

Preparations of bases for amphibious forces: http://www.history.navy.mil/library/online/comnaveu/comnaveu-5.htm#part3

US Army Center for Military History – Exercises
http://www.history.army.mil/documents/WWII/beaches/bchs-7.htm

National Archive Sources:
WO 219/4873 – Training exercises 1st US Army
WO 199/1390 – Exercises 'Duck'
WO 199/2318 – Exercise 'Trousers': Stores and equipment
WO 205/474 – Exercise 'Fabius': Operational orders and instructions
WO 199/2317 – Exercise 'Trousers': Third Canadian Infantry Division
WO 199/2322 – Exercise 'Tiger': US Forces
WO 219/187 – Demonstrations, exercises and rehearsals: programmes and schedules
US National Archive Sources:
http://research.archives.gov/search?expression=slapton&pg_src=brief&data-source=online
US Ducks & Trucks; Slapton Sands dwellings evacuated Royal Marines & sailors train US Army at Dartmouth, 01/10/1944
National Archives Identifier: 76272 – Local Identifier: 428–NPC-1933
Joint Army & Navy amphibious manoeuvres, Slapton Sands, Devon, England, 02/14/1944
National Archives Identifier: 76060 – Local Identifier: 428–NPC-1545
Joint Army & Navy amphibious manoeuvres, Slapton Sands, Devon, England, 02/14/1944
National Archives Identifier: 76061 – Local Identifier: 428–NPC-1546
Joint Army & Navy amphibious manoeuvres, Slapton Sands Devon, England, 02/14/1944
National Archives Identifier: 76059 – Local Identifier: 428–NPC-1544
Training amphibious manoeuvres, Slapton Sands, ENG, 03/17/1944
National Archives Identifier: 76109 – Local Identifier: 428–NPC-1631
US Army & Navy landing manoeuvres, Slapton Sands, ENGLAND, 01/08/1944
National Archives Identifier: 76270 – Local Identifier: 428–NPC-1929

Critical Past:
United States troops board a landing craft in England as a part of a manoeuvre during World War II.
http://www.criticalpast.com/video/65675051453_United-States-troops_Landing-Ship-Tank_men-at-beach_vehicles-unload
American soldiers being given personal gear as they prepare for invasion of France
http://www.criticalpast.com/video/65675051444_American-soldiers_personal-gear_convoy-of-jeeps_loading-supplies_military-jeeps
Army half tracks being loaded into nose section of US LST (Landing Ship, Tank) at Dartmouth, England during World War II.
http://www.criticalpast.com/video/65675060435_Landing-Ship-Tank_army-half-tracks_prior-to-invasion-of-France_World-War-II
M-7 HMCs being loaded onto US LCT (Landing Craft, Tank) at Dartmouth, England during World War II.
http://www.criticalpast.com/video/65675060436_Landing-Craft-Tank_tanks-driven-into-landing-craft_invasion-of-France_troops-on-board
British and American troops practise amphibious assaults at a beach near Dartmouth, England
http://www.criticalpast.com/video/65675066889_Allied-troops_amphibious-landing_practise-landing_Landing-Craft-Vehicles

**Chapter 11**
1. Colin John Bruce, *Invaders*, Caxton Editions 1999, page 121
2. Ian Gardiner and Roger Day, *Tonight We Die as Men*, Osprey Publishing 2009, page 80
3. Stephen E. Ambrose, *Band of Brothers*, Touchstone, New York 1992, page 57
4. Gardiner and Day, *op.cit.* page 80
5. Alex Kershaw, *The Bedford Boys*, Simon & Schuster 2003, page 84
6. Laurent Lefebvre, *They were on Omaha Beach* 2003, page 22/23
7. Lefebvre, *op.cit.* page 48
8. Lefebvre, *op.cit.* page 58
9. Lefebvre, *op.cit.* page 68
10. Kaufman and Kaufman, *op.cit.* page 10
11. Kaufman and Kaufman, *op.cit.* page 29
12. Russell Miller, *Nothing less than Victory – the Oral History of D-Day*, Pimlico 2000, page 14
13. Miller, *op.cit.*
14. Gardiner and Day, *op.cit.* page 98
15. Miller, *op.cit.* page 39 (Sergeant John R. Slaughter, D Company, 1st Battalion, 116th Infantry)

**Chapter 12**
1. Nigel Lewis, *Channel Firing: Tragedy of Exercise Tiger*, Viking 1989, page 272
2. The figure quoted on the Exercise Tiger Memorial at the Arlington National Cemetery in Arlington, Virginia is 639. Charles B. MacDonald quotes 749 in 'Slapton Sands: The Cover-up That Never Was' on the US Naval History and Heritage Command Website http://www.history.navy.mil/faqs/faq20-2.htm
3. Lewis, *op.cit.* page 265
4. http://www.channel5.com/shows/revealed/episodes/the-secret-d-day-scandal-revealed and http://dday7.channel4.com/ Channel 4 d-day as it happens
5. Richard T. Bass, *Exercise Tiger*, Tommies Guides, 2008, page 144
6. Torbay and South Devon District Council: 'We do not hold any coroners' files for Torbay dated earlier than 1949. As far as we are aware, no files from before this date were

preserved in Torbay.' http://www.devon.gov.uk/index/councildemocracy/record_office/
information_about_devon_heritage_services/guide_sources/coroners__records_in_devon.
htm#torbayandsouthdevon

7. Alex Kershaw, *The Bedford Boys*, Simon & Schuster, 2003, page 84
8. Lewis, *op.cit.* page 249
9. J.E. Kaufmann and H.W. Kaufman, *The American GI in Europe in World War II*, Stackpoole
   Books, 2009, page 27
10. *Ibid.*
11. *Ibid.*
12. *Ibid.*
13. Amphibious Operations Invasion of Northern France Western Task Force June 1944, chapter
    II, Naval Gunfire http://www.ibiblio.org/hyperwar/USN/rep/Normandy/Cominch/
    Neptune2.html
14. WO 199/2318 Exercise 'Trousers': Stores and equipment

Chapter 13

1. *Western Morning News*, 29 July 1944
2. WO 32/11065 – Training: General (Code 35(A)): Training areas, airfields and habitable
   houses, held under Defence Regulations relinquished
3. *Ibid.*
4. *Ibid.*
5. *Ibid.*
6. *Western Morning News*, 25 August 1944

War Transport Advisory Committee Members:
Mr W.G. Jerwood, chairman; R.D. Blight, sub-district manager, Ministry of War Transport,
Totnes area; J.R. Bradford, Bradford Sand and Haulage; W.Efford, cattle haulier; H.C.
Glasson, Great Western Railway; W.H. Grimley, district transport officer, Ministry of War
Transport, Plymouth; R. Jackson, Devon War Agricultural Committee; E.F. King, Plympton
Trading Co; C.H. Knapman, Erme Milling Co. Ltd; T.H.L. Luckes, cattle haulier; C.W.
Northcott; Messrs F.T. Clarke and M.D. Downs, Kingsteignton; J. Owen, J.Owen Ltd;
F.White, sub-district manager, Ministry of War Transport; W.F.F. Bishop, secretary, 11 Mill
Street, Kingsbridge.

7. *Western Morning News* 29 July 1944
8. *Western Morning News* 4 August 1944
9. WO 205/492 Fire support in an assault on a heavily defended beach, vol. I

General principles governing support by naval gunfire:
Accuracy of fire primarily depends on the accuracy with which the ship's position can
be fixed. With the most modern aids to navigation the average error in position will be
approximately 200 yards, in any direction.

If air observation of fall of shot is available (it must be assumed that no ground observation
will be possible at this stage) this error and any uncorrected ballistic errors, will be evident
from the fall of shot of the opening salvos and can be corrected. Thereafter 50% of the shots
should fall within an area about 200 yards square with either 6" or 15" guns at all ranges
and this accuracy should be maintained without the necessity for spotting more than an
occasional salvo.

If no observation of the fall of shot is possible, with the above accuracy of navigation the overall probable error of the mean point of impact will be of the order of 400 yards. During the Sicilian campaign the average error of the initial salvos of a number of 6-inch shots at long range was about 400 yards.

If the target is visible from the sea, and in the absence of smoke, a measure of direct observation will be possible and the accuracy will vary accordingly. In a few cases, e.g. against a battery sited on rising ground, will the accuracy approach that to be expected from the air of FOO observation. Generally speaking the latter conditions will not exist on the French coast. When FOOs have landed and are in position to observe the accuracy of both, the off-shore fire should be considerable and comparable to that of land artillery.

10.  http://www.goldendays.org.uk/reg-hannaford-2/
11.  *Devon and Exeter Gazette*, Friday, 2 February 1945

### Chapter 14
1.  *After the Battle,* Number 45, 1994, 'The Tank that missed D-Day'
2.  Captain Harry C. Butcher USNR, *My Three Years with Eisenhower,* Simon and Schuster, New York, 1946, pages 527–9.
3.  Armor in operation Neptune (Establishment of the Normandy Beachhead). A Research report prepared by committee 10, officers' advanced course, the Armored School 1948–91
4.  J.E. Kaufmann and H.W. Kaufman, *The American GI in Europe in World War II*, Stackpole Books, 2009, page 48 (Staff Sergeant E. Gibson, Company A, 70th Tank Battalion)
5.  Kaufman and Kaufman, *op.cit.* page 46 (Corporal Wardell Hopper Company B 741st Tank Battalion)
6.  *The West Australian*, Monday, 9 July 1945, 'Unseen Army – Devon People's Sacrifice'
7.  *Western Morning News*, Saturday, 13 May 1950
8.  *Western Morning News*, 25 Nov 1950, 'Mines and bomb removed from Slapton Sands'
9.  *Western Morning News*, 30 Nov 1950, letters to the editor
10.  US Navy Landing Craft Tank (Rocket), personal recollections of Lt Commander L.W. Carr USN http://www.combinedops.com/US%20LANDING%20CRAFT%20ROCKET.htm
11.  *Ibid.*
12.  http://warchronicle.com/16th_infantry/soldierstories_wwii/wozenski.htm
     Imperial War Museum, Sound Archives, Edward Wozenski interview in two parts, accession numbers 3014/2/1 and 014/2/2
13.  *Western Morning News*, 24 March 1950, 'Rocket Missile found at Slapton Sands – Postmaster gave it a tap'

# Index